MADE TO shine

A Girl's-Only Devotional

by

THE SONFLOWERZ

Becca Leander Nicholson & Elissa Leander Tipps

Discovery House.
from Our Daily Bread Ministries

To our parents, Don and Thea Leander.

Mum and Dad, you have given us a lifetime of support in our calling to write and encourage others—even traveling with us for more than ten years as we ministered in music! You raised us in a home filled with biblical truth, real grace, and the love of Father God. You are our greatest blessing and now our dearest friends. We thank you for making this devotional what it is.

Made to Shine: A Girls-Only Devotional

© 2016 by Becca Leander Nicholson and Elissa Leander Tipps

All rights reserved.

Discovery House is affiliated with Our Daily Bread Ministries, Grand Rapids, Michigan.

Requests for permission to quote from this book should be directed to: Permissions Department, Discovery House, P.O. Box 3566, Grand Rapids, MI 49501, or contact us by e-mail at permissionsdept@dhp.org.

All Scripture quotations, unless otherwise indicated, are taken from the Holy Bible, New International Version®, NIV®. Copyright © 1973, 1978, 1984, 2011 by Biblica, Inc.™ Used by permission of Zondervan. All rights reserved worldwide. www.zondervan.com. The "NIV" and "New International Version" are trademarks registered in the United States Patent and Trademark Office by Biblica, Inc.™

Scripture quotations marked AMP are from the Amplified® Bible, Copyright © 1954, 1958, 1962, 1964, 1965, 1987 by The Lockman Foundation. Used by permission.

Scripture quotations marked ESV are from The Holy Bible, English Standard Version® (ESV®), copyright © 2001 by Crossway, a publishing ministry of Good News Publishers. Used by permission. All rights reserved.

Scripture quotations marked HCSB are from the Holman Christian Standard Bible®. Copyright © 1999, 2000, 2002, 2003, 2009 by Holman Bible Publishers. Used by permission. Holman Christian Standard Bible®, Holman SCB®, and HCSB® are federally registered trademarks of Holman Bible Publishers.

Scripture quotations marked MSG are from *The Message*. Copyright © by Eugene H. Peterson 1993, 1994, 1995, 1996, 2000, 2001, 2002. Used by permission of Tyndale House Publishers, Inc.

Scripture quotations marked NLT are from the *Holy Bible*, New Living Translation, copyright © 1996, 2004, 2007, 2013 by Tyndale House Foundation. Used by permission of Tyndale House Publishers, Inc., Carol Stream, Illinois 60188. All rights reserved.

Cover and interior design by Kris Nelson/StoryLook Design.

ISBN: 978-1-62707-499-5

Printed in the United States of America

First printing in 2016

Contents

This Is for You

So you want to be noticed? Don't we all. We want to be the girl strutting her stuff down the halls of the school, the girl everyone turns to see. We want to be the one with the contagious smile and perfectly timed joke—that girl. We resonate with the idea of shining so brightly. Even if you say you like to stay back in the crowd, unnoticed, I bet there's a hint of curiosity inside. Who has *never* wondered, "What would it be like to stand out?"

Who could you be if you really did shine?

The qualifications for being a standout chick aren't entirely clear. Do we have to be popular or the prom queen? Do we need natural charm or a line of boyfriends at our door? Not exactly.

Everything hinges on what you shine for. Is it for popularity and personal fame?

I shine for God. He's the One who created us to shine. "You're here to be light, bringing out the God-colors in the world," Jesus said. "God is not a secret to be kept. We're going public with this, as public as a city on a hill. If I make you light-bearers, you don't think I'm going to hide you under a bucket, do you? I'm putting you on a light stand. Now that I've put you there on a hilltop, on a light stand—shine! Keep open house; be generous with your lives. By opening up to others, you'll prompt people to open up with God, this generous Father in heaven" (Matthew 5:14–16 MSG).

There's a boldness about light, a defiance against the dark. So it is with those who shine.

When I was fourteen, I wrote my first song, and woven throughout were the themes of shining, purpose, ambition, and Jesus. "Use Me" was rough, and even though I never sing this song anymore, I suddenly remembered the lyrics as Becca and I wrote this book. You'll see why:

> *To shine on this earth is to be noticed for what you live by.*
> *I cry to shine forth, for my Savior, who gives me life.*
> *Lord, shine me in the dark.*

Since that time, I've had a boundless love of songwriting, playing guitar, and singing. Although I wasn't a great musician then (I didn't sound like I belonged on *The Voice)*, "Use Me" and other songs like it spurred me to start a band. They were the reason I went on the road, too. It was all because of a message: We shine because of God's light within us. It has nothing to do with our outside appearance or the stuff we have!

Without a connection to Jesus, shining is impossible. Shining starts with a real relationship with Him. And then He sends His Spirit to guide us through this life as His light-bearers. Without the Holy Spirit we are helplessly stumbling in the dark, trying to find the light switch. We can't actively shine without God's help.

And so begins the challenge to welcome the Source of light— Jesus Christ and His Spirit—to flow through you each day. Come on a journey with Becca and me. Take each chapter, each page of this book as an invitation to find out what the best life can look like.

It's not easy, but completely worth it. As your sisters in Christ, we dare you to go for it! We're with you.

Elissa
The Sonflowerz

P.S. We've created a unique playlist for each day in *Made to Shine*! From our own music libraries, we've chosen our favorite songs that will make a perfect soundtrack as you read. You can find this awesome music list on our website, sonflowerz.com/madetoshine. You might decide to download these songs and take a listen at the end of each day's reading. Or, if you are like Becca, you'll probably turn up the tunes as you read the devo. You can purchase songs on iTunes or choose to stream them. Either way, by the end of the book you'll have the most amazing music library ever!

Day 1
Your Canvas

by Becca

I literally gasped when I saw this story on the news.

The alarm was raised in room 17 of London's National Gallery after an assistant spotted a man spraying two paintings with an aerosol can. Brilliant works from the 17th century, now completely covered in red spray paint! Though Nicolas Poussin's paintings had survived centuries, a trigger-happy fool destroyed them in a moment.

Now imagine that God—the essence of who He is—could be captured in a portrait. All of us carry a canvas of God in our mind's eye, a painting of His character. But like those paintings in the museum, our portrait of God can be marred by our life experiences.

For Hailey, it was her parents' divorce that altered the canvas. The day her dad walked out, never to return, put a deep smear across her understanding of who God really is. Margaret lost her house in a fire when she was eight and her big sister ran away from home when she was ten. These experiences created smudges that disfigured Margaret's view of God. Both girls thought, "Will *God* leave me too?"

What words would you use to describe God?
If He were painted on a canvas,
what would His *eyes* say to you?
DESCRIBE:

• Powerful

• friendly

• welcoming

• intense

• forgiveness

We all desperately need to find the true picture of God.

Humans keep adding to the canvas, spraying over God's image with lies and letdowns. By a stroke, a spray, a mark with their own cans of aerosol, they hide the one-of-a-kind masterpiece. Then it's hung in a public gallery and the masses make a verdict: God is angry, disappointed, or uninterested. All the while, God's true face is hidden beneath.

But God is real, and *He* should have the final say on who He actually is.

Here's the truth: We see God when we see Jesus. He is the untarnished picture of God, on display! Jesus revealed to the world how infinitely God loves us.

Jesus answered . . .
"Anyone who has seen me has seen the Father."
JOHN 14:9

The paintings in the museum were swiftly cleaned by hand under a microscope. Then they were proudly put back for public display. Aren't we overdue for some restoration work on our damaged portraits of God?

Friends, it's time to allow the steady hand of God's Son, Jesus Christ, to chip away the drips and wipe away the stains. You may very well find that the true picture of God is more beautiful than you would ever have imagined.

As a middle-school kid, I handed over the brush as Jesus painted the picture of God in my heart. I experienced God's love for the first time at youth camp. As I watched my friends worship and connect with God, the atmosphere stirred me and something powerful took place. I was captured.

When my sister and I began the journey of becoming The Sonflowerz, writing songs and singing together, it became our mission to share this truth with other girls: "We look at this Son and see the God who cannot be seen. We look at this Son and see God's original purpose in everything created" (Colossians 1:15 MSG).

Reflection & Action

1. What experience in your life has helped to define your view of God?

° Going to Christian
Life Church
° Teen Girl group
° Sunday School

2. Read Ephesians 3:16–19. Ask Jesus to reveal to you the true character of God.

PER·SPEC·TIVE [per-spek-tiv] the proper
or accurate point of view or the
ability to see it; objectivity

For in Christ all the fullness of the Deity lives in bodily form.
Colossians 2:9

In the beginning was the Word, and the Word was with God,
and the Word was God. He was with God in the beginning.
John 1:1–2

"Edge of My Seat"
by The Sonflowerz

The Daily Song is each day's special soundtrack. These are songs written and recorded by us, The Sonflowerz! You can download them on iTunes and find lyrics to sing along with us at Sonflowerz.com.

Day 2
Up Close and Personal

by Elissa

Ever seen storytelling from a felt board? These are my earliest, most classic memories of Sunday school. My teacher, Mrs. Bowling, used little felt characters to act out Bible stories. Somehow this (literally!) fuzzy interpretation of Jesus, Mary, Joseph, angels, and donkeys made the stories come alive.

From those stories, I realized that people walked for miles to hear Jesus teach. Imagine that! Whatever their background or lifestyle, they were sincerely drawn to Him. Jesus made God more real—not only to the people He encountered, but to me and my friends right there in Sunday school. In the words He spoke and the way He loved some down-right messed-up people, we saw that God truly cares about *us*.

Today, my understanding of Jesus goes far beyond a felt board cutout. He isn't just someone I read about, He is—through the Holy Spirit—living in my heart.

It's truly amazing. How did this change happen within me?

It goes back to when I first picked up a guitar. Attempting to play those first songs was so frustrating. I couldn't get anything down for months. But then I began to disconnect from the struggle and simply sang out my thoughts to God as I played a simple chord. While I was playing, God's Holy Spirit—His presence that we can't see with our eyes but can feel with our heart—brought me comfort, peace, and joy. It was as if a soft breeze swept over me. And right then I experienced what it is to know God personally.

Because He loves us, Jesus gave His life when He died on the cross. When I think of a love that big, I can hardly grasp it! He knew that our sin, the way we miss the mark God sets for us, separates us from God. Jesus could have prevented His own death, but instead He chose to die in our place to pay the price for our wrongs. He was willing to do everything it took to draw us close to the Father.

Jesus was willing
to do everything it took
to draw us close to the Father.
Everything!

The Bible is like a love letter that God wrote to us. And here's a line from that letter that reveals something amazing: "Because of His great love for us, God, who is rich in mercy, made us alive in Christ even when we were dead in transgressions—it is by grace you have been saved" (Ephesians 2:4–5). Think of that!

As I got to know Him better, the way I know my family and friends, I fell in love with Jesus. It didn't feel like work—I *wanted* to know Him! I discovered and developed a personal relationship with Jesus by spending time with Him in simple prayer and by digging into the New Testament. And I always loved singing my songs to Him.

You can't have a true relationship with someone by knowing him or her from a distance—you have to connect in a real way. That's the kind of relationship God wants with you. He longs to make himself known to you each day, whether you find Him through music or Scripture or a prayer while you're riding your bike. The key is taking time to connect with Him.

Reflection & Action

1. Is Jesus more to you than stories you've heard? List all the things Jesus is to you:

_____

_____

_____

_____

_____

_____

_____

_____

_____

_____

2. Talk to God about your desire to connect with Him in a real way, and to experience the love He has for you.

CON·NEC·TION [kuh-nek-shuhn]
part, link, bond, relationship,
circle of friends

"For God so loved the world
that he gave his one and only Son,
that whoever believes in him shall not perish
but have eternal life."
John 3:16

Praise the LORD. Give thanks to the LORD,
for he is good; his love endures forever.
Psalm 106:1

"My Heart Is Alive"
by The Sonflowerz

"My Heart Is Alive" Song Story by Becca

This song started with a text message from Holland! In the midst of a routine radio interview, the DJ asked if we'd be up for a "fun challenge." He used the word *fun*, but all I could think was *crazy*: Would we write a song in 20 minutes, then play it on the air—*live?*

Every week this station challenges a band to write a song based on text messages listeners send in. Why not, right? We had only a few minutes to come up with lyrical genius, inspired by the phrase "start of a bright day", sent in from a European smart phone. Elissa grabbed her guitar, while I dug in my purse for a pen and notebook.

My competitive nature kicked into gear, and before the commercial break ended we had the start of a bright song! Nailing it on the air was another story. . .

Day 3
Promise Keeper

by Becca

One confused girl wrote to me, "I don't understand. My boyfriend said he would always love me. Now he laughs at me in front of his friends."

Promise is defined as an assurance that someone will do a certain thing. It's a stated guarantee that a particular thing will happen. And promises come at us from all directions.

Political candidates vow, once they are in charge, to save the planet. TV commercials try to convince us to buy carpet cleaners, diet pills, and electronic gadgets that never work. Friends—boy and girl—make plenty of promises, too.

The world is full of promise makers and promise breakers. But what ever happened to promise *keepers?*

Think about the reliability of the morning sun or how the stars always fill the sky at the end of each day (even the cloudy ones!). Picture the ocean's strong tide and the moon's consistent glow. All of these point to our ultimate Promise Keeper.

I love this passage: "Don't put your confidence in powerful people; there is no help for you there. When they breathe their last, they return to the earth, and all their plans die with them. But joyful are those who have the God of Israel as their helper, whose hope is in the LORD their God. He made heaven and earth, the sea, and everything in them. He keeps every promise forever" (Psalm 146:3–6 NLT).

The night before He died on the cross, Jesus prayed passionately in a place called the Garden of Gethsemane. He asked God the Father if He could somehow avoid the extremely sad and painful hours ahead of Him. But then Jesus said, "Yet not as I will, but as you will" (Matthew 26:39), and faithfully chose death on the cross for us.

Faithfulness isn't just something God *has*; it's who He *is*. Jesus Christ is the same yesterday, today, and forever (see Hebrews 13:8).

But betrayals come at us from every angle—the friend who sides with the popular crowd instead of you, the guy who shoves you away, the parent who leaves without saying good-bye. With this kind of wounding, it's easy to build skepticism toward everyone around us. We may even begin to doubt God too. But despite the unfaithfulness of others—or even our own—God's love for us never changes. The rough times we experience are perfect opportunities for our trust in God to grow stronger. He is trustworthy, even if no one else is.

Faithfulness isn't just
something God has,
it's who He is.

For the girl who had been disrespected by her ex-boyfriend, I wrote back with my favorite passage about God: "Though the mountains be shaken and the hills be removed, yet my unfailing love for you will not be shaken nor my covenant of peace be removed" (Isaiah 54:10). A covenant is a heartfelt agreement, a vow—and God is speaking it to us!

Truth fears no questions.

Is there a situation in your life, good or bad, that has influenced your view of God, the Promise Keeper?

JOT IT DOWN:

One of His most marvelous promises is that Jesus is coming back for us. "My Father's house has many rooms," Jesus told His disciples, "if that were not so, would I have told you that I am going there to prepare a place for you? And If I go and prepare a place for you, I will come back and take you to be with me, that you also may be where I am" (John 14:2–3). In the book of Revelation, it says that in heaven, Jesus is called "Faithful and True" (19:11).

Through His Holy Spirit, Jesus won't leave your side when you've been disappointed by others. No one else can keep a promise like God. He is the ultimate Promise Keeper.

Reflection & Action

1. Ask God to reveal and to heal the hurtful experiences that might prevent you from trusting Him.

2. Read Psalm 37 and write down each promise from God to you in that chapter.

FAITH·FUL [feyth-fuhl] true to one's word, reliable, dependable, trusted

"'He will wipe every tear from their eyes.
There will be no more death' or mourning or crying or pain,
for the old order of things has passed away."
Revelation 21:4

I sought the LORD, and he answered me;
he delivered me from all my fears.
Psalm 34:4

"Like No One Else"
by The Sonflowerz

Day 4
Love Letters

by Elissa

For a while I'd been feeling like reading my Bible was just one more thing on my daily to-do list. I wore that badge of achievement proudly, having read the Bible cover-to-cover many times. *I know what it says,* I thought, *and God can always remind me of Scripture when I need Him to.* It's not as if I never read it. I just wasn't in it every day.

And I was in a dark place of sorts. For weeks, my voice had been frail, so frail I could barely sing. It was scary for me, because I had a lineup of important trips on my calendar. I changed my diet, hoping it would help. I was taking medicines and vitamins, and praying—a lot—to get my voice back.

Then a crazy thing happened to me. I left on a trip to lead worship in Pennsylvania. Once there, I felt like the speaker was talking just to me.

She began by telling her story. As a victim of an attack in college, she had found herself desperate for God to rescue her from daunting fears that plagued her every day.

How did she climb out of this dark place? The Word of God soothed and restored her. She read in Hebrews 4:12, "The Word of God is alive and active. Sharper than any double-edged sword, it penetrates even to dividing soul and spirit, joints and marrow; it judges the thoughts and attitudes of the heart."

God was speaking to me through this woman's testimony, and it was revolutionary. Yeah, I'd been missing something in my diet—God's Word! The speaker went on to read Deuteronomy 8:3, which says, "Man does not live on bread alone but on every word that comes from the mouth of the LORD."

So if I need more than bread to live, and I'm not eating God's Word every day, then I must be malnourished!

How would your body feel if you didn't eat anything for days? Well, that's what I was doing to my spirit by not reading the Bible regularly.

Suddenly, I knew that reading the Bible wasn't just a job to get through. It was a necessity for life and for my healing.

Back then, if I could have rated my daily Bible intake on a scale of one to ten (one being the lowest), it would definitely have been around a three. My spirit was starving, and I hardly knew it.

I've heard it said...

We become what we read.

How would you describe *your* Bible intake right now?

When you read the Bible, you will discover God's marvelous pursuit of humanity. You'll see how He created us to be in a love-filled relationship with Him, but how people chose other gods besides Him. Page after page tell how God still pursued us with love.

Jesus is the pinnacle of God's love chasing us down. And we encounter what that love is like in Scripture. When we read the Bible, we begin to see ourselves in its pages. Words jump out to us, speaking right into our need.

On flight home from the East Coast, I made plans to carve out time every day to open up a chapter in the Bible. In the weeks that followed, God restored my voice. But more importantly, I discovered the power of His Word to change me from the inside out.

Reflection & Action

Find a Bible translation that speaks your language. There are outstanding study Bibles with maps, pictures, and all kinds of explanations to illuminate what is said. (Becca is into the New Living Translation right now, but I often read the New International Version as well as The Message.)

Think about this … if we divide the Bible into text messages, with each one being 60 characters, then God has sent you 22,103 text messages!

MAL·NOUR·ISHED [mal-noor-ishd] lacking the proper amount of food for growth and good health; poorly supplied with vital elements

For the word of the LORD is right and true; he is faithful in all he does.
Psalm 33:4

Your word, LORD, is eternal; it stands firm in the heavens.
Psalm 119:89

DAILY SONG

"Nothing to Fear" by The Sonflowerz

Day 5
I Heard God Speak

by Elissa

One of the defining moments of my life occurred when I heard God speak for the first time. My very best friends had just turned their backs on me. I was a lonely, heartbroken twelve-year-old. Crying myself to sleep, I prayed for God to give me good friends I could count on.

And right there, in my lowest moment, I heard Him whisper in my heart, "I will bring you friends, and the first one will be named Amanda." I considered this strange, immediately doubting that these thoughts could be God's—but I waited to see.

A couple weeks later, a new girl arrived in my sixth-grade class. Her name was, astoundingly, Amanda. Some may call it coincidence, but my young heart was overwhelmed by God's careful attention to my simple prayers.

Shortly after that, my family moved across country. *Well, that was convenient,* I thought. *Now I have to start over finding friends?* Saying good-bye to my hometown was an all-time low. I got into our moving van trying to hide my apprehension.

When we arrived in Colorado, I practically stepped out of that van to meet my first friend. She was also named Amanda. (Of course!) This "Amanda" thing was pretty cool. Just another confirmation that the message I'd heard was truly from God.

So how do we hear God's voice? He speaks to us primarily through the Bible, but His Spirit has a direct line to our hearts.

When have you heard God speak to you?
RECORD IT:

_____

_____

_____

_____

_____

_____

_____

_____

_____

_____

_____

You can probably guess that there are things that keep us from hearing God speak. Willingly giving in to sin is a big hindrance. Sometimes we have to do a 180, turning away from other things in order to hear from God. Being too busy to spend time with God is another major roadblock. He needs our attention, time, and our fullest trust to speak into our lives.

God invites us into conversation every day!

People talk about having a "soft heart" toward God to help us learn to hear His voice. A soft heart has no walls surrounding it, and no limitations on what God can say. What if God asks something that requires you to change or bend to His design? A hard heart would hold up a stop sign telling God not to come any closer. But by His nature, God always longs to be in closer communication with us.

John's gospel confirms that Jesus, who knows us intimately, also intends to be known by us: "I am the Good Shepherd. I know my own sheep and my own sheep know me. In the same way, the Father knows me and I know the Father.... [My sheep] recognize my voice" (John 10:14–16 MSG).

When God spoke to me about Amanda, it was a life-changing moment. But it caused me to realize that He had been speaking to me long before that time, in much more subtle ways—a beautiful sunset, my mom's hugs, a pick-me-up through Scripture, or the thrill of answered prayer. God invites us into conversation every day.

And now you know. You *can* hear the voice of God.

Reflection & Action

1. Are your prayers two-way conversations? Take a minute to ask God to help you hear His voice. It may not be instantaneous, but you can start by learning to listen for Him as you pray.

2. Listening to Scripture and to God's voice speaking to your heart, what might God be saying to you today?

CON·VER·SA·TION [kon-ver-sey-shuhn]
informal interchange of thoughts
and information

*"This is G*ᴏᴅ*'s Message, the God who made earth,*
*made it livable and lasting, known everywhere as G*ᴏᴅ*:*
'Call to me and I will answer you.
I'll tell you marvelous and wondrous things that
you could never figure out on your own.' "
Jeremiah 33:3 (MSG)

I will instruct you and teach you in the way you should go;
I will counsel you with my eye upon you.
Psalm 32:8 (ESV)

"Beautiful Miracle"
by The Sonflowerz

Day 6
Flip the Switch

by Elissa

Have you ever seen the reality TV show called *Buried Alive?* It's about people who have overloaded their houses with junk. So much junk that they can't get around from room to room. On the show, it's not uncommon for homes to be stacked to the ceiling with unopened Christmas presents and boxes from online shopping orders.

Buried Alive sends in a cleaning team, each person wearing rubber gloves and a mask. Why? Because these miracle workers often uncover black mold on the walls and insects rummaging through trash.

And people *live* in this!

As I watched one episode unfold, the homeowner was extremely emotional, even indignant, as volunteers helped sift

through the waist-high clutter. She didn't want to see the ugly mess and deal with it. For her, keeping things as they were was security.

A false kind of security.

We often feel safe in familiar surroundings, even if our surroundings are harmful piles of trash! *Buried Alive* got me thinking about my own life. Are there dark, dirty rooms inside me filled with boxes and garbage? If our hearts are anything like a house, there are probably rooms that need attention.

Fear. Sin. Regret. Guilt. Pain. What room in your heart's house might contain some of this clutter from your past?

Maybe I've cracked open a door once or twice and thought, *This is too much to handle. I'll deal with it some other time.*

But even if I could find enough courage to tackle the disarray, at the end of the day, I can't fix up my own heart. The mess still exists.

This search for righteousness—or a clean heart—can be endless. Trying to get my heart right isn't something I can navigate on my own.

When you became God's child, He gave you a Helper to take care of this cleaning. The Holy Spirit is inside you to help you live a life that shines from the inside out. As a result, the cleanup can really begin! It's God's Spirit who leads you into all truth, shedding light on your sin and any area in need of attention (John 16:13).

The Holy Spirit is inside of you
to help you live a life that shines
from the inside out.

Girl, you and I need some light! What would happen if you flipped the switch on in every room of your internal house? Ask God to help you see what spaces need attention and how to start the process of living wholeheartedly for Him.

It's not about putting things in order by yourself, but instead letting God have His way in you. His intention is to do all the heavy lifting, but we need to choose to live our lives in His light, instead of ignoring our problem spaces. "If we walk in the light, as he is in the light, we have fellowship with one another, and the blood of Jesus, his Son, purifies us from all sin" (1 John 1:7).

Don't get caught buried alive! What our hearts hold on the inside really matters. When we offer our mess, God accepts us and turns the whole situation around.

I've heard it said...

Faith is the strength by which a shattered world shall emerge into the light.
—Helen Keller

Reflection & Action

1. The dilemma isn't whether or not you have a messy room; we *all* do. Have you flipped the switch to expose it to the Light? Ask the Holy Spirit, our Counselor, to help you shine light in every dark place of fear, sin, regret, guilt, or pain.

2. Find an older mentor or a parent to pray with you about this area of your life where you have committed to see change. Write down a name in the space below.

_____

3. Remember: The cleanup is directed and accomplished by God, in His grace, His power, and His timing. Turn your ear to His voice during the process.

LIGHT [lahyt] something that makes things visible, illumination source

May God himself, the God of peace,
sanctify you through and through.
May your whole spirit, soul and body be kept
blameless at the coming of our Lord Jesus Christ.
The one who calls you is faithful,
and he will do it.
1 Thessalonians 5:23–24

You, Lᴏʀᴅ, keep my lamp burning;
my God turns my darkness into light.
Psalm 18:28

"Love Walked In" by The Sonflowerz

"Love Walked In" Song Story by Elissa

I'm a songwriter at heart and whenever I'm picking up a guitar, I'm writing! But there was a solid year when I couldn't finish a single song. I tried and tried, but found myself, in December, wondering if I had completely lost my touch.

Then it happened. I was walking through my house one cold winter night and a drip from the bathroom faucet caught my attention. Some might call a drip "annoying"—but that night it was inspiration! I heard a beat and even a melody in that drip. In an instant, I had my guitar in hand to compose.

My husband saw that the door was shut, and heard music echoing down the hall. He knew a new song was coming into being! I wrote about our hearts being like a house, where God can fill every room, and "Love Walked In" made it onto the page.

Then I got online to find a Scripture. It was a verse I knew from memory, but I needed to search its actual reference. Suddenly, my web browser brought up a news headline: a shooting had just happened in Connecticut. *Not another shooting,* I thought, heart-broken. The bridge to this song was written in response:

Into the grieving, Love walked in.
Into the empty, Love walked in.
Into the dying, You ran in. . . .

I love the idea of Jesus "running in." He ran in for all of us when we were dying in our sin. When He gave His life on the cross, He met every need we could ever have.

Day 7
Borrowed

by Elissa

I was happily engaged and waiting for a fantastic wedding day. I had no idea that my fiancé, Chad, was busy preparing for our new life together by selling off his beloved piano. When he told me the piano was gone, I gasped. (But his sacrificial choice paid for our honeymoon.)

Once we were married, I was shocked by my husband's enthusiastic ability to let go of things. As newlyweds we had loads of empty space in our house. Not a lot of stuff to our name, and yet I would find Chad giving away computers, guitar gear, and books. I could barely contain my knee-jerk reaction to chase after the folks he was generous to—and take back the things he gave away.

I wonder how many times I've sung these words to God

during a church service: "It all belongs to you." In 1 Chronicles 29:11, King David praised God by saying, "Yours, LORD, is the greatness and the power and the glory and the majesty and the splendor, for *everything in heaven and earth is yours*" (emphasis mine).

If everything is God's, does that mean *nothing* is mine?

I'm overwhelmed by the urge to preserve what I have, maintain control, and protect what's in my possession. This just highlights my need to know God better. He's not out there to squash my joy in life; He's here to provide for me like a good Father. But at the same time, He is a Dad who wants His kids to be free of self-centered, self-satisfying, greedy ways.

Take a look at the things you've collected over the years: from the priceless heirlooms to the so-called junk. A stockpile of Christmas gifts, dusty Barbie dolls, heaps of clothes. Do any of these things hold onto you? Do the things you own, own you?

Give yourself a rating from one to ten—with one being "I love giving stuff away" and ten indicating "I'm always afraid God will ask me to give something away":

Whatever your answer, you are not alone. For me, I have to admit, it's difficult to let go. But the narrow, often challenging path of a Christ-follower includes living open-handed before God, with a heart like clay (or maybe Silly Putty!), moldable in His hands. Your heart doesn't have to attach itself to the stuff you have; you can find your treasure in God. He is enough.

I'm in the process of believing all God's promises for me. He guarantees us some pretty amazing things. But while I'm on this journey, I pray that my heart would rest in His love and not be wrapped up in stuff. I'm fully aware that "where my treasure is, there *my heart* will be also" (Matthew 6:21 paraphrased).

Everything in
heaven and earth
belongs to God.

Shortly after my husband gave away his piano, a marvelous thing occurred. A family friend told us he needed a place to store his gorgeous grand piano. While our friend is overseas for years with the military, we are the proud caretakers of this exceptional instrument. What a gift from God!

Today when I saw this beautiful piano in my house, I paused and prayed, "God, you are in control of my desires, and everything I have is yours. It's all borrowed from you. Thank you for each gift. And help me to remain willing to give just like you do."

Reflection & Action

1. Read Romans 8:32 and journal what it means to you.

_____

_____

_____

_____

_____

_____

_____

_____

_____

_____

2. How crazy would it be to take the word "mine" out of our vocabulary? Try it for a day!

TREA·SURE [tre-zher] valuable things, to regard or treat as precious

"Give, and it will be given to you.
A good measure, pressed down,
shaken together and running over,
will be poured into your lap.
For with the measure you use,
it will be measured to you."
Luke 6:38

A generous person will prosper;
whoever refreshes others will be refreshed.
Proverbs 11:25

"Crazy Love"
by The Sonflowerz

Day 8
President's Daughter

by Becca

Ever wonder why no one in the Bible has a last name like us? You have Paul, David, Esther, and Mary, but where's that last name? The best we get is "Saul son of Kish"! No reference to a Mr. Saul McDonald.

When I was beginning the fourth grade, I was transferred to Tomas Rivera Elementary—a small school in the heart of Texas. The building was so new I could smell the fresh paint and carpet when I walked in for the first time.

Our neighborhood had been assigned to this new school, and many parents were not thrilled about their kids being forced to move. My parents were in the same boat, so they decided to get involved. Even though he was already busy running a business, my dad offered to start the school's first Parent-Teacher Association.

The PTA kickoff meeting was held in the school auditorium, where I noticed a table with name tag stickers and black Sharpie markers. Grabbing a tag for myself, I wrote, "Daughter of Don Leander—PTA President." Apparently, I didn't care if people knew my own name or not. I was the daughter of the president.

Slapping the nametag on my shirt, I left the table confident that my dad was the president. Every word that came out of my nine-year-old mouth, even the way I treated people in the room, was a direct result of this confidence.

Now imagine that school auditorium is your life. Who are you? What would you write on your own name tag? Take a second to fill in this blank with a list of characteristics that first come to mind:

I AM:

There is an identity out there greater than any personal description or family name. Your ultimate worth has been given to you by Jesus Christ. *This* is what makes you a daughter in God's family. "Praise God for the privilege of being called by His name" (1 Peter 4:16 NLT).

> There is an identity
> out there greater
> than any family name.

Are any of the characteristics you wrote down like your own parents? My dad and I are similar in a lot of ways. (Just ask my mom!) Yet my heavenly Father is the one who truly defines me. We can simply fill in the blank with, "I am His."

There are all kinds of labels that we give ourselves. But God wants to strip away every label until we see ourselves completely as daughters of God.

Some days I forget the privilege of being called "His." I'm trying to be someone I'm not, or I get bogged down in chasing popularity. My need to belong to something worthwhile is strong. But Jesus has put an end to this longing—we belong to Him.

It's as if He's saying, "First and foremost, you are my daughter. Don't think too much about your identity elsewhere; I want you to know that your identity is wrapped up in me."

Eventually, after that night years ago, my excitement about being called a president's daughter awakened me to my true identity. I am the *King's* daughter. "To all who did receive him, to those who believed in his name, he gave the right to become children of God" (John 1:12).

Reflection & Action

1. What aspect of your family's name and identity has helped you? What has boxed you in?

_____

_____

_____

_____

2. Why do you (or don't you) feel like part of God's family?

_____

_____

_____

_____

_____

3. Ask God to reveal your born-again status as His daughter, so that you live out this belief today: "I am HIS."

I·DEN·TI·TY [ahy-den-ti-tee] **the unique characteristics of a human being; individuality**

See what great love the Father has lavished on us, that we should be called children of God! And that is what we are! The reason the world does not know us is that it did not know him.
1 John 3:1

"I took you from the ends of the earth,
from its farthest corners I called you.
I said, 'You are my servant';
I have chosen you and have not rejected you.
So do not fear, for I am with you;
do not be dismayed, for I am your God.
I will strengthen you and help you;
I will uphold you with my righteous right hand."
Isaiah 41:9–10

"Now That I Am Yours"
by The Sonflowerz

Day 9
Who He Says I Am

by Elissa

My mom has carried a piece of worn-out paper in her Bible for years. It's a list of Scriptures declaring who we are in Christ. When I faced difficult, teary-eyed moments in my life, she would whip out this paper and begin reading it to me: *You are a child of God* (Romans 8:16); *you are a new creation in Christ* (2 Corinthians 5:17); *you are forgiven* (Colossians 1:13–14); *you are complete in Christ* (Colossians 2:10). My mom told me that she prayed these thoughts over me, too. Photocopied a bazillion times, her list is now in my own Bible, in my suitcase, and by my bed.

Sometimes I'm guilty of forgetting who God says I am. Wherever I go, whatever I'm doing, I need a reminder of who I am because of Jesus.

Wrap yourself in the thought that He calls you His daughter.

While we were making one of our CDs, I found myself wondering if my singing was even worth recording. I'm often given opportunities to perform, but then I question if I have what it takes to get on the stage.

It's only when I sit down with the words God speaks about me—the kinds of words my mom collected on her list—that all of these negative thoughts disappear!

God went to great lengths to send His Word to us. Through the prophets of old like Isaiah and Jeremiah, through the New Testament apostles like Paul and Peter, and ultimately by sending His very Son, Jesus, to speak His message, God has sent His truth to us in a passionate way. When you think about what He did, how does that make you feel?

Insecurity can't hang around long in the heart of a child of God. We are not left to struggle through life alone. We are not given tasks too big to handle (even when we *feel* overwhelmed). We walk day by day with the Creator of the world! With Him, all things are possible (Matthew 19:26) and we are cared for completely. Wrap yourself in the thought that God calls you *His* daughter. He treasures you as His own.

Believe this:
You are the adored girl of God. (John 3:16)

You are His chosen servant (John 15:16) and you are given gifts from His heart in order to glorify Him (Ephesians 1:3). You are delivered from darkness (Colossians 1:13), and more than a conqueror (Romans 8:37). You are holy and without blame before Him in Christ (Ephesians 1:4). The list doesn't stop there, but I'm running out of paper!

> Wherever I am,
> I need to be reminded
> of who I am because of Jesus.

The key to knowing your identity is to agree with who God says you are. If this is hard to do, tape a verse on your mirror and read it to yourself every morning until it settles in!

His words, not ours, have the final say. Even when we forget and make mistakes, we can look up and remember again, *I am a dearly loved daughter of God.* Nothing can change this reality. Every day we have a new chance to live it.

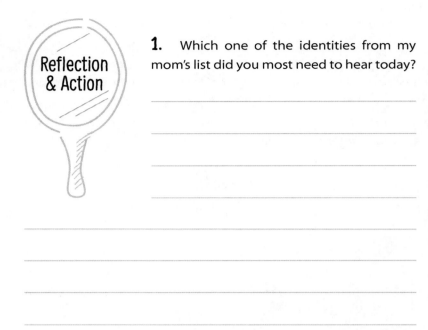

Reflection & Action

1. Which one of the identities from my mom's list did you most need to hear today?

_____

_____

_____

_____

_____

_____

_____

_____

_____

_____

2. Take a minute and ask God to help you walk out your real, God-given identity.

COM·PLETE [cuhm-pleet]
having all necessary
elements; total

Therefore, as God's chosen people,
holy and dearly loved,
clothe yourselves with compassion,
kindness, humility, gentleness and patience.
Colossians 3:12

Don't you know that you yourselves are God's temple
and that God's Spirit dwells in your midst?
1 Corinthians 3:16

"Dearly Loved"
by The Sonflowerz

Day 10

2508

by Becca

The number jumped out from the page. Christine was stunned as she read the paperwork that arrived by certified mail.

She had found out a year earlier that she was adopted, and had begun a search for more information on her birth parents. But she was shocked to discover that there was no record of her birth mother giving her a name. According to the official record, she was "number 2508"—like a pass code or a house number. Her birth mother's lack of personal attention—she didn't even name Christine before giving her away!—felt unbelievably hard.

For Christine Caine, who tells this story in the book *Undaunted*, the revelation of 2508 translated into "unwanted." She felt

Baby #2508

herself slip into despair. That number had power to discourage and dampen her soul.

Perhaps you've faced some difficult realization yourself. Whether you read something, or recalled something that happened in your past, or heard someone say something that really hurt, your heart has fallen into a hopeless spiral of unworthiness.

Maybe the accusation is even closer than a person or a document. Perhaps it comes through your own voice. As you look into the mirror you hear it. The moment you make even the slightest mistake—or just see someone who seems to have it all together—the voice condemns you: *Ugly. Stupid. Accident-prone. Failure.*

The reality is that we've *all* heard—and often believed—lies about ourselves. The words fester within us, mocking us every time we come up short or feel unworthy.

I've heard it said...

The average person thinks 1,200 unconscious negative words per minute.

But negative words from your past don't have to define you today . . . or shape your future. God has spoken the deepest truth about who you are throughout the pages of Scripture. And when held up to the light of what God says about you, the lies simply don't stand. It's a matter of choosing who you'll believe.

What's better than spending hours learning to hula-hoop, or play Risk, or touch your tongue to your nose? Practicing how to think the truth about yourself! And the Bible is packed with verses that tell you that God made you, knows you, loves you, and wants the best for you.

As tears streamed down Christine's face, she flipped open her Bible out of desperation. Feeling a nudge that she knew came from God, Christine opened to Isaiah 49:1 (NLT), which says, "The

Lord called me before my birth; from within the womb He called me by name."

Like a warm drink on a bitter cold night, Isaiah's experience comforted Christine. It exposed the lie even as the adoption report began to settle into her mind. Unwanted? No. She was *chosen*.

God has spoken the deepest truth
about who you are
throughout the pages of Scripture.

Who will you choose to believe? Christine could have believed—because her birth mom decided not to keep or even name her—that she was unlovable, unwanted, and unworthy. The course of her entire life would have changed. But because she threw those papers away, picked up her Bible, and let the words of her heavenly Father go deep into the crevices of her heart, she was transformed into a fearless girl of God.

Christine believed God. And that changed everything.

Reflection & Action

1. Sticky notes are my favorite. Use them to write down Scriptures that encourage you, and post them where they're visible as you get ready in the morning.

2. Look up these Scriptures and fill in the blank:

Ephesians 1:4—I am:

_____

John 1:12—I am God's:

_____

1 John 4:10—I am:

_____

3. Change your speech! Your body, soul, and spirit listen to every word that's spoken, by others and by you. Most of the time, we *become* what we hear. Consider what you speak about yourself each day, and ask God to help you change your speech to reflect truth.

CHO·SEN [choh-zen] selected; marked for special privilege

"As the Father has loved me, so have I loved you.
Now remain in my love."
John 15:9

"Then you will know the truth,
and the truth will set you free."
John 8:32

"Little Lies"
by The Sonflowerz

"Little Lies" Song Story by Becca

My husband was a touring guitarist for our church's worship leader. It was an exciting time when he took me on the road one week! We were at a church in Oklahoma, worshiping with everyone who had gathered.

At one point, I walked into the foyer and found a cute little girl, about five years old, sitting alone on a couch. Her mom was across the room. I decided to sit down next to her as she played with her purse.

The girl's mom allowed me to take her little princess into the auditorium, where the music was happening. When a fast song started, I motioned for the girl to dance with me. What kid doesn't want to dance? I can't count how many of our performances have included kids dancing in the front row!

She took my hands and we twirled a couple times. But she suddenly let go and rushed to slump back into a chair. I was sad. She seemed to be uncomfortable with people watching her.

I wondered why a small child would be self-conscious. Had someone ever said something rude about her appearance, or had she developed negative thoughts on her own? I know that happens with many girls—they begin to believe lies, lies that keep them from enjoying life as precious children of God.

"Little Lies" is the song I wrote for this girl—but the truth is, *all* of us need the reminder.

Day 11
Irreplaceable

by Becca

Rummaging through an old dresser, I found it. The vibrant oranges, blues, and pinks hadn't faded much. I pulled mom's old blouse out from the dresser and admired the hand stitching.

With its vintage patterns and beautiful lace, I instantly fell in love with the top. Mom wore it as a British hippie in the 1970s. The lady who sold it to her said it had been made from an antique bed spread!

My first chance to wear the blouse onstage was at a summer festival near the Great Lakes. A mom and her daughter greeted me afterwards, eager to know where I shop. I smiled and told the story of my well-traveled top. Later I grabbed a hot dog, loaded it with mustard, and thought, "I'd better eat this carefully. I'll never find another shirt like this!"

When was the last time you discovered something vintage, one of a kind . . . *irreplaceable?* Perhaps it's hanging in your closet or has a special place in your room.

Did you know that God considers *us* His irreplaceable treasures? How do I know this? Each one of us is so precious to God that He was willing to give up what He loved most. Imagine what it must have felt like for the Father to give His only Son on our behalf. It's impossible to fully grasp how deep is the Father's love for each one of us.

And God carefully thought through every detail when He created you. The writer of Psalm 139 says:

"How precious are your thoughts about me, O God.
They cannot be numbered! I can't even count them;
they outnumber the grains of sand!" (verses 17–18 NLT).

We get another glimpse of God's thoughts about us from Ephesians 2:10 (NLT, emphasis mine):

"For we are God's *masterpiece.* He has created us
anew in Christ Jesus, so we can do the good things
He planned for us long ago."

There is no second copy of you—even if you were born a twin! You are significant to God's plan for humanity. You are not in any way average or ordinary.

God specifically designed your qualities, look, and style. He gifted you with purpose like no one else. What's one way you can thank God for how He's created you? By being you! Acting like other people or comparing yourself to others are not things God had in mind for you. You owe it to yourself to be yourself!

You owe it to yourself to be yourself!

When I wore that vintage blouse that summer, I was clothed in something irreplaceable. Unique. Only one was ever made. How amazing! Now I understand how my Father sees me.

Yes, me. Yes, you.

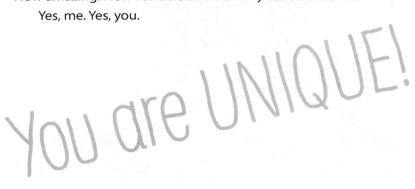

You are UNIQUE!

Reflection & Action

1. For me, the shirt is a reminder of how irreplaceable I am. Do you have some special object that symbolizes this for you? If not, can you create a reminder of some sort? Then find a way to display it!

2. Extend this truth to someone else. Today, share this idea with a friend who may be forgetting she's irreplaceable too.

U·NIQUE [yoo-neek] the only one; without equal

For he chose us in him before the creation of the world to be holy and blameless in his sight. In love he predestined us for adoption to sonship through Jesus Christ, in accordance with his pleasure and will—to the praise of his glorious grace, which he has freely given us in the One he loves.
Ephesians 1:4–6

"Are not two sparrows sold for a penny? Yet not one of them will fall to the ground outside your Father's care. And even the very hairs of your head are all numbered. So don't be afraid; you are worth more than many sparrows."
Matthew 10:29–31

DAILY SONG

"More Than I Think I Am" by The Sonflowerz

Day 12
Beauty Lessons

by Becca

Growing up, I never really liked my hair. I envied those girls in the magazines who had shiny, smooth locks. Because I couldn't compete with what they sported, I decided to hide my frizzy hair in a ponytail. To make matters worse, I was unsuccessful in all my attempts to cover up my terrible acne! All I could see in photos were my flaws.

Anyone relate?

The truth is, all of us can think of something about our bodies that we dislike. I didn't like my hair and acne-prone skin. Someone else doesn't like her nose. Another girl doesn't like her hips.

It's so easy to get stuck in this destructive thinking. We see beauty in other people, but not in ourselves.

Why? Did God make a mistake? Before you answer, check out this passage in the book of Psalms:

"You created my inmost being;
you knit me together in my mother's womb.
I praise you because I am fearfully and wonderfully made;
your works are wonderful, I know that full well"
(Psalm 139:13–14).

My feelings toward my so-called imperfections made me wonder how I could ever see myself the way God sees me. There are still flaws I mentally list when I look in the mirror. But now I take that list to God in prayer—along with all the stuff I feel insecure about—and it becomes my own modern-day psalm.

Does the image in the mirror consume your thoughts?

True beauty isn't surface-level. But deciphering exactly what true beauty is becomes a tricky thing when Facebook selfies and fashion magazines put such a focus on external appearance.

That kind of thinking triggers comparisons, compromising our inner beauty when we try to impersonate the "top model." Genuine *inner* beauty is difficult to uncover on Instagram and Facebook, don't you agree?

Genuine inner beauty
is difficult to uncover
on Instagram and Facebook.

Almost two thousand years ago, the apostle Peter wrote this in a letter that hits hard even today: "Don't be concerned about the outward beauty of fancy hairstyles, expensive jewelry, or beautiful clothes. You should clothe yourselves instead with the beauty that comes from within, the unfading beauty of a gentle and quiet spirit, which is so precious to God" (1 Peter 3:3–4 NLT).

Former supermodel Jennifer Strickland has a powerful story about how God changed the way she thinks about herself. She wasn't the "perfect picture," though on the outside you might have thought so. Even as a model, Jennifer was always unhappy with herself. She attempted to fill her emptiness and loneliness but she never could. Her endless striving to be a perfect weight (which doesn't exist), get noticed by guys, and compare favorably with other models brought her to her knees. She left the modeling world and never turned back. "God has given me a purpose," she says, "to share His love, to tell the stories of my life that display so powerfully the beauty that God sees in the heart of every woman."

Here's a true beauty secret I've discovered: a stunning brilliance from inside is unveiled as we know Jesus more and more. He will transform the way we see ourselves when we glimpse how radiant we look to Him! That knowledge will fill every empty place—the kind that Jennifer felt and the kind that I've felt. With His love and acceptance, we will shine with God-given beauty from the inside out.

I've heard it said...

People who worry about their hair all the time, frankly, are *boring.*
—Barbara Bush

Reflection & Action

1. Describe someone you know who is beautiful *on the inside.* What makes that person so attractive?

_____

_____

_____

_____

_____

_____

2. How concerned are you about your appearance? Could this keep you from connecting with Jesus?

_____

_____

_____

_____

_____

_____

LOVE·LY [luhv-lee]
exquisitely beautiful

Those who look to him are radiant;
their faces are never covered with shame.
Psalm 34:5

Charm is deceptive, and beauty is fleeting;
but a woman who fears the LORD is to be praised.
Proverbs 31:30

DAILY SONG

"You Captured Me"
by The Sonflowerz

Day 13
Miss Understood

by Elissa

Recently I was at Rudy's, my favorite restaurant for good BBQ. While standing in the dessert line, trying to decide between peach cobbler and banana pudding, a family in front of us began to debate. Loudly. I couldn't help but notice a teen girl carrying a massive diaper bag—helping her mom—while two younger siblings ran in circles around her.

It happened like clockwork. The four-year-old swung back her leg and wacked her older sister full force in the shin. The teenager winced in pain and gave her little sister a slap. Like falling dominoes, the baby in the mother's arms began to cry. And the four-year-old began to whine.

The mom suddenly began to yell and curse at the oldest sister. In the mother's view, the teenager was to blame. At this point, the dad jumped in, shouting, "That's it!

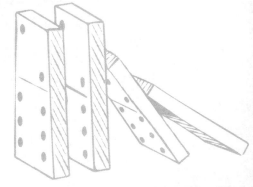

I'm done with this!" Then he stormed out of the restaurant. Now the mom shouted at the teen, "You've ruined everything! He's never coming back and it's all your fault!"

Blamed. Accused. Rejected.

Imagine being on trial, unable to plead your case before the judge hands down a guilty verdict. How terribly lonely it would be to feel like everyone is against you! We weren't meant to carry our burdens alone.

After I left Rudy's, I felt remarkably grieved for this family . . . especially the teenager, carrying such a weight on her shoulders (literally and figuratively). I wonder how many of you can relate to her?

There is a well-known person who was often misjudged. He lived an extraordinary life revealing the mysteries of God to people. It was common to find Him sharing a meal and conversation with the misfits and outcasts of society. When He would leave a room, people were left scratching their heads. "Who was that?" they thought, "and what was He saying?"

This man is Jesus. He ultimately paid the penalty of a criminal, though He was innocent in every way.

Here's a description of Jesus from the prophecy of Isaiah:

"Surely he took up our pain and bore our suffering,
yet we considered him punished by God,
stricken by him, and afflicted. But he was pierced
for our transgressions, he was crushed for our iniquities;
the punishment that brought us peace was on him,
and by his wounds we are healed" (Isaiah 53:4–5).

The punishment that brought us peace was on Him? Here's a Man who can recognize a heavy burden! He understands any opposition or loneliness we may struggle with (Hebrews 2:18). And yet we find Him saying, "Get away with me and you'll recover your life. I'll show you how to take a real rest. Walk with me and work with me—watch how I do it. Learn the unforced rhythms of grace. I won't lay anything heavy or ill-fitting on you. Keep company with me and you'll learn to live freely and lightly" (Matthew 11:29–30 MSG).

I've heard it said...

Put your expectation on God, not on people.

We aren't meant to carry burdens alone.

If you're linking arms with Jesus, things aren't going to be perfect—but you'll always make it to the other side. He gets you. He knows the burden you're lugging around, and He has promised never to leave you (Hebrews 13:5).

With Him, you will make it through anything.

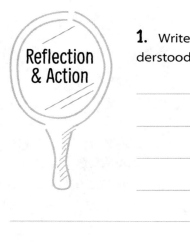

Reflection & Action

1. Write about a day when you felt misunderstood.

_____

_____

_____

_____

_____

_____

_____

_____

_____

_____

2. Spend a few minutes talking with God about that day, right now.

UN·DER·STOOD [uhn-der-stuhd]
thoroughly familiar with

I lift up my eyes to the mountains—
where does my help come from?
*My help comes from the L*ORD*,*
the Maker of heaven and earth.
Psalm 121:1–2

For our light and momentary troubles are achieving for us
an eternal glory that far outweighs them all.
So we fix our eyes not on what is seen,
but on what is unseen, since what is seen is temporary,
but what is unseen is eternal.
2 Corinthians 4:17–18

"Like a Flood"
by The Sonflowerz

Day 14
At the Center

by Elissa

Holding a bowl of popcorn, I plopped myself down on the beanbag chair. Five of my closest friends and I were in my best friend's bedroom for a slumber party. Her mom had brought up a few board games and snacks—but all we wanted to do was stay up and talk! Our laughter filled the room and overflowed into the rest of the house . . . until one girl brought up the subject of *boys*. We all got quiet and listened as she shared about her secret crush.

All of us would begin junior high after the summer. New school and teachers, but the same classmates we'd known in elementary. That meant Blake, Ally's new crush, would be there too.

For the first time, I had to really think about dating—what my opinion would be about that sort of thing. Especially when Ally and Blake ended up hold-ing hands the first week of school. *What?*

To find "the man of your dreams," everyone says you've got to "follow your heart." Movies portray romances that are driven by emotions and surprising events where true love is the ultimate result. The couple walks into the sunset, and then the credits roll! Who hasn't watched a Disney princess movie? But are those sto-ries realistic?

God has a lot to say about your "love story." In fact, He cares about *every* detail of your life, even more than you do.

The words in Proverbs 3:5–6 (ESV) became a life verse for me:

> "Trust in the LORD with all your heart,
> and do not lean on your own understanding.
> In all your ways acknowledge him,
> and he will make straight your paths."

I gave God full control over my life, especially my decisions about boys. As I lived out the words in Proverbs 3, being open to God's voice with all of my heart, He directed my life. It turned out that dating during junior high and high school wasn't what God wanted for me.

Throughout those years, God was busy sculpting my inner beauty—you know, teaching me patience and humility, helping me become a better friend and sister, preparing me for the hus-band He had in mind.

But before you picture me alone on Friday nights, sitting at a table for one, let me just say those "singleness years" were *far* from boring. They were actually the most exhilarating time of my life! Snowboarding trips, late nights hanging out with my best girl friends, writing songs, and traveling consumed any free time I had.

But as great as those things were, the most incredible part was how my relationship with God flourished. He gave me such confidence to be who I was made to be. I saw a clearer picture of God's calling on my life and how I could serve Him through music.

We are enough without a boyfriend.

You are enough without a boyfriend. Adding a boy to your life doesn't complete you—*only God does* (Colossians 2:10). You can be confident that you are never alone, because your friend-ship with God is for all eternity. He's even with you moment by moment, as you walk your school hallways, open your books to study, or lie in bed.

I love how David prays in Psalm 139, "I'm an open book to you [God]; even from a distance, you know what I'm thinking. You know when I leave and when I get back; I'm never out of your sight. You know everything I'm going to say before I start the first sentence. I look behind me and you're there, then up ahead and you're there, too—your reassuring presence, coming and going. This is too much, too wonderful—I can't take it all in!" (Psalm 139:2–6 MSG).

Remember my junior-high friend Ally? It wasn't long before she came to me with a broken heart. For the rest of the school year, she and Blake sat at opposite sides of the classroom, avoiding each other with an awkward sense of rejection.

I've heard it said...

Anything worth doing is worth doing *right*.

. . . .

I took note that I didn't want break ups to plague my life. I wanted the peace and promise of Jesus to overflow inside me. With Jesus, not boys, at the center of every-thing, my life and yours have incredible possibilities!

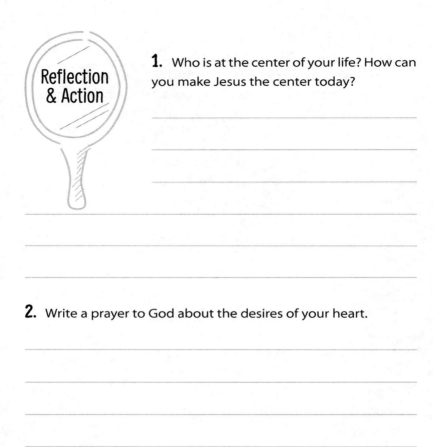

Reflection & Action

1. Who is at the center of your life? How can you make Jesus the center today?

2. Write a prayer to God about the desires of your heart.

CEN·TER [sen-ter] the point from which an activity or process is directed, or on which it is focused.

I waited patiently for the LORD;
he turned to me and heard my cry.
He lifted me out of the slimy pit,
out of the mud and mire;
he set my feet on a rock
and gave me a firm place to stand.
He put a new song in my mouth,
a hymn of praise to our God.
Many will see and fear the LORD
and put their trust in him.
Psalm 40:1–3

Because of the LORD's great love we are not consumed,
for his compassions never fail.
They are new every morning;
great is your faithfulness.
I say to myself, "The LORD is my portion;
therefore I will wait for him."
The LORD is good to those whose hope is in him,
to the one who seeks him;
it is good to wait quietly
for the salvation of the LORD.
Lamentations 3:22–26

"Always Reign"
by The Sonflowerz

Day 15
The Ring

by Elissa

Every girl has a thing or two to say about the wedding ring she wants. My minimal input to my fiancé's pick was precise and it was my grandma who really set the tone for my wedding ring choice.

She gave me my first "real" ring, a small, 14 karat gold band with a heart in the center. When she was a teen, her father had given it to her as a purity ring. The significance was huge to me. Grandma had cancer and knew she didn't have much time left when she gave me the ring. Her gift came with a purpose: I was to wear it as a reminder of what God's Word says about purity.

Rings are often a symbol of commitment. For me, this precious gold ring from Grandma communicated a clear message: I belong to Jesus, every part of me—my heart, mind, and body.

Purity is a word we use to describe how we are "set apart" to God. In the Old Testament, we read about God choosing Israel as a people set apart for Him. From the tribes of Israel, He chose one called the Levites to be even more separate. They were the priests who ministered before God in His holiest place, the temple, for hundreds of years.

You and I are called to be set apart, to be holy to God, as well. 1 Peter 2:9 says, "you are a chosen people, a royal priesthood, a holy nation, God's special possession, that you may declare the praises of him who called you out of darkness into his wonderful light."

As followers of Christ, we have a life that is exciting, full of fulfillment and love. God's love is perfect, unlike anything else in this world! But being a Christ-follower demands something of us: full surrender. Our lifestyle should look so different from the world's that people stop and ask, "What's she got that I don't have?" Because we want to honor God with our bodies and minds, people may even wonder, "Why is she so peculiar?"

You are called
to an extraordinary life,
which is opposite to the
patterns of the world around
you most of the time!

You are called to an extraordinary life, which is opposite to the patterns of the world around you most of the time! Accepting this calling is what shining is all about.

1 Corinthians 6:19–20 says:

"Do you not know that your bodies are temples of the Holy Spirit, who is in you, whom you have received from God? You are not your own; you were bought at a price. Therefore honor God with your bodies."

There are so many decisions to make every day. If we want to live set apart to God—if we want to honor Him with our bodies—we can only do that through the power of God's Holy Spirit living inside us.

Rings, necklaces, and other special things can only serve as a reminder of your commitment. God is looking for your heart's devotion, your surrender to His plan for your life. When you say "yes" to God's best, you can be sure His grace will come alongside to help you do it. Matthew 5:6 gives us this promise: "Blessed are those who hunger and thirst for righteousness, for *they will be filled*" (emphasis mine).

Friend, if no one else has called you to this, let me be the first. *Will you start fresh today and commit to a no-regrets life of purity?*

When he proposed, my husband placed a sparkling diamond ring on my finger. That diamond was the very same one my grandmother had worn on her wedding ring all her life. I see Grandma's diamond every day. Her legacy of full-on commitment to Christ is the thing I want to be remembered for too.

Will you start fresh today and commit to a no-regrets life of purity?

Reflection & Action

1. Write down your own prayer to God, describing your desire to aim your life toward purity.

2. What family member or other person in your life can you tell about your commitment to purity?

OP·PO·SITE [opp-uh-zit] contrary or radically different in some respect, as in nature, qualities, direction, result, or significance; opposed

*Therefore, since we are surrounded by such a great
cloud of witnesses, let us throw off everything that
hinders and the sin that so easily entangles.
And let us run with perseverance the race marked out for us,
fixing our eyes on Jesus, the pioneer and perfecter of faith.
For the joy set before him he endured the cross,
scorning its shame, and sat down at the right hand
of the throne of God.
Hebrews 12:1–2*

*How can a young person stay on the path of purity?
By living according to your word.
Psalm 119:9*

"Offering My Life"
by The Sonflowerz

Day 16
Made New

by Elissa

Missy pounded the bathroom counter with her fist. "I did it again!" she said in frustration. Looking into the mirror, she saw teary eyes and messy hair, a reflection that accurately represented her inner state. Missy had just fought with her mom about the most trivial things—again. It seemed like every time Missy was asked to help around the house, she would explode. Of course, she wanted to be loving and gentle, but inside she was uptight and bothered. It was getting harder to forgive herself for these reactions.

Have you ever felt that way? Frustrated with yourself and needing to move forward, but frozen with regrets?

A few years ago, I glimpsed a picture of the kind of grace that Missy's heart longed for. I was walking in my sacred place, which happens to be a path that lines the shores of southern England. I was captivated by the waves crashing on shore. The salt water rolled back and forth to reveal perfect silken sand.

As I breathed in the cool fresh air, I pondered this beautiful shoreline. What the waves do for that shore is a picture of what the blood of Jesus does for us. His death on the cross gives us a completely new beginning.

> Your past mistakes
> don't define you—
> or your future.

Just as the waves wash the shore of any old footprints, so believing in Jesus erases our failures and mistakes. He is the One who has removed our sins from us as far as the east is from the west (Psalm 103:12). Not only did Jesus' sacrifice secure our eternity with Him, His blood washes us every day, every minute, leaving us blameless in God's eyes. Yes, blameless!

Romans 8 is my favorite chapter in the Bible. It affirms that we are no longer under the power of sin and shame: "With the arrival of Jesus, the Messiah . . . those who enter into Christ's being-here-for-us no longer have to live under a continuous, low-lying black cloud. A new power is in operation. The Spirit of life in Christ, like a strong wind, has magnificently cleared the air, freeing you from a fated lifetime of brutal tyranny at the hands of sin and death" (Romans 8:1–2 MSG).

Your past mistakes don't define you—or your future. Regrets don't need to plague your thoughts.

Jesus Christ has made you a completely *new* person to live in the fullness of His righteousness (Colossians 2:10).

I've heard it said...

It's not as important how we start but how we finish.
—Joyce Meyer

> "Therefore, if anyone is in Christ,
> the new creation has come:
> The old has gone, the new is here!"
> (2 Corinthians 5:17)

Your search for approval and perfection can end! Jesus has met all of God's standards on our behalf—He is the perfect One. Now we can find refuge in the all-sufficient grace of God. We are fully accepted no matter how we might feel from one day to the next.

Reality is, we are *made new* through Christ. So now we should start living like it!

Missy approached her mom with humility. "I'm sorry," she said. Beginning fresh in her own heart meant she could take steps in mending her relationship with her mom too.

Having grace for yourself, as well as for others, is essential to shining for God. When we do this, I'm sure our Father in heaven smiles.

Reflection & Action

1. Write a journal entry about any regrets you have. Ask God to show you how to surrender those regrets to Him.

_____

_____

_____

_____

_____

_____

2. Read Matthew 26:26–28, the story of the first act of Communion. Finding a quiet place, ask God to remind you of the amazing sacrifice Jesus made so you could be free. Because of Jesus' sacrifice for you, you have been made entirely acceptable to God (2 Corinthians 5:21).

3. Maybe you would like to take communion on your own time, with a sip of grape juice and a cracker, to remember the death of Jesus. Or maybe you will join in communion soon at your church. Either way, remembering what Christ has done should become a regular habit!

GRACE [grayss] the free and unmerited favor of God, as shown in the salvation of sinners and the giving of blessings

He predestined us for adoption to sonship through Jesus Christ, in accordance with his pleasure and will—to the praise of his glorious grace, which he has freely given us in the One he loves. In him we have redemption through his blood, the forgiveness of sins, in accordance with the riches of God's grace that he lavished on us.
Ephesians 1:5–8

Brothers and sisters, I do not consider myself yet to have taken hold of it. But one thing I do: Forgetting what is behind and straining toward what is ahead, I press on toward the goal to win the prize for which God has called me heavenward in Christ Jesus.
Philippians 3:13–14

"Cover Us"
by The Sonflowerz

Day 17
1,000 Bouquets

by Becca

When my dad came to tell me I'd had a delivery, I skipped every other stair to get there as fast as I could. On the piano was a slender box addressed to me. I bent back the lid to reveal a red bouquet. Roses? Who had sent them? I searched for a name but only found a card that read "To Rebecca." Astonishment and intrigue brought me to a point of giddy excitement. I arranged the roses in water and called all my friends, hoping they could reveal the mystery.

But still no answer.

I spent the rest of the evening racking my brain. There was no boyfriend. No admirer that I knew of. I began to wonder if the flowers had come to the wrong address—though they definitely had my name on them!

Have you ever received a gift like this? How did it make you feel?

Flowers on the doorstep are traditionally meant to say "I love you." But within a week, this beautiful gift began to wilt. And just as flowers fade, chocolates are devoured, and teddy bears stuffed in a closet. Over time, the good feeling those gifts bring dwindles away. We feel empty again.

Feelings of love can come and go. One moment we are blissfully romanced and the next we are shrouded in longing. Our feelings can flicker like a candle in the wind. But there is one place where the joy is sustained. It's in the love God embodies. It's the love that He *is*.

Long before you could ever do anything for Him, God made the statement, "I love you." He has given us the gift of His love and scattered clues everywhere!

> Before you could prove anything
> or do anything for Him,
> God made the statement, "I love you."

So what is so extraordinary about this love? Can it top a dozen roses?

One time, after we had played a concert in Eagle Point, Oregon, we packed our car for a four-and-a-half-hour drive to catch a plane home. On the way out, our host, Cyndi, told us about a stop we might want to make on the way to the airport. It was a place that people would drive hours to see, she said.

A tulip farm. Yep.

About three hours later we turned off the interstate. A small sign pointed the way down a dirt road. We turned in, pulling up to a man waiting in a booth. He was asking five bucks for parking.

By this time we were all eager to see what we'd been trying to picture in our minds. Would it be worth the price of parking? We walked to the top of the next hill, and there it was.

Rows of tulips for *miles*. Every color and variety you could dream up! These were nothing like store-bought tulips. They were more than twice the size! I thought for a split second that I had walked into another world, a scene described in fairy tales.

Like other visitors who had found this treasure off the beaten path, we marched up and down each row, occasionally crouching down for pictures. My eyes had never seen so many colors in one place. I breathed in the fragrance.

Before long, our flight beckoned, and we made our way back to the parking lot. I thought back to those roses delivered to my door years earlier. Next to these acres of floral beauty, a modest bouquet paled in comparison. My roses, though a kind and thoughtful gesture, were simply a borrowed bouquet. God, the creator of everything, owns the fields. He is the author of true beauty—including the colorful, fragrant flower of love.

Do you know you are "be-loved"? Created to *be loved*. God goes public in Jeremiah 31:3: "I have loved you with an everlasting love; I have drawn you with unfailing kindness."

I glanced back at those fields a final time. They seemed endless. No fence in sight. Then it dawned on me: that's how to describe God's love for us. It's limitless.

God's love isn't a theory.

God's love isn't a theory. Like the tulips I could see and feel and smell as they danced in the wind, God's love is a reality. He demonstrated this profound love in Jesus (see Romans 5:8). Far beyond the temporary rush of a bouquet of flowers, God's love promises an eternity of beauty and happiness.

To this day I don't know who sent me those roses. But I know who created the roses . . . and I know He loves me perfectly.

Reflection & Action

1. Next time you run across a field of wildflowers—or even see a bouquet of flowers—spend a minute to breathe in their fragrance. Remember God's love for you.

2. Read 1 Corinthians 13:4–8. Where you read the word *love,* insert *Jesus.* Have you ever read it this way before?

_____

_____

_____

_____

_____

_____

If you're like me, you need a kick start to get you opening the Word in the morning. Start with Ephesians 1, which sets the stage for understanding God's love for you. It's one of my favorites.

EV·ER·LAST·ING [ev-er-lass-ting]
never coming to an end,
eternal

"I have made you known to them,
and will continue to make you known
in order that the love you have for me may be in them
and that I myself may be in them."
John 17:26

But you, Lord, are a compassionate and gracious God,
slow to anger, abounding in love and faithfulness.
Psalm 86:15

But because of his great love for us, God,
who is rich in mercy, made us alive with Christ
even when we were dead in transgressions—
it is by grace you have been saved.
Ephesians 2:4–5

"Speechless"
by The Sonflowerz

Day 18
Dream Life

by Elissa

I was walking with my mom on a well-worn jogging path by the neighborhood creek. Not far off, a family approached us from the other direction. Three kids were barreling toward us on bikes so we scooted over to give them more room.

Two older brothers led the way. A young girl with cherry-red cheeks was doing everything in her power to keep up with them. Her long, curly locks were flung back by the wind, and the set of training wheels keeping her upright bounced over the gravel.

We got a good look as she whirled past us, and then I glanced back. *How cute,* I thought. Suddenly she threw back her head and shouted out in triumph, "I'm living the *dream* life!"

My mom and I giggled . . . and giggled some more. Long after the family was out of sight, we were still talking about this exuberant little girl.

What is the dream life anyway? Her words stuck with me, and their timing was perfect.

I had been so tangled up with worry that the here and now was beginning to feel like grunt work. Each day, all I could think of was the huge pile of stuff I had to do. But the dream life isn't about those things. I had actually lost sight of the dreams that mattered to me.

What's your idea of a dream life?

JOT IT DOWN:

It's as if Jesus was speaking right to me when He said, "Give your entire attention to what God is doing right now, and don't get worked up about what may or may not happen tomorrow. God will help you deal with whatever hard things come up when the time comes" (Matthew 6:34 MSG). In other words, don't worry about tomorrow.

But worry was what my mind had been stuck on—until this bike-riding wake-up call appeared.

What about you? There are decisions to make. Who will you invite to your next party and will you choose to befriend the kid who's always the outcast? Or in a few years the questions will be about college and finding a job or a place to live. At some point, you might be making a choice about who to marry. Does worry fill these spaces in your life?

I've
heard
it said...

**The future belongs to those who believe in the beauty of their dreams.
—Eleanor Roosevelt**

Now I know why Jesus told us not to worry about our future: the way we're wired, fears and dreams for the future can easily swallow up our present joys.

What if I told you that you are living your dream life *now?* Can you see yourself, like that five-year-old, shouting out, "I'm living the dream life!"? (Try it now: 1 . . . 2 . . . 3 . . . Go!) Now that you've yelled out loud and spooked the dog, here are the essential elements:

When Jesus taught His followers to be like little children (see Matthew 18:3), He was wanting us to trust the Father completely. "Seek first *his* kingdom and *his* righteousness," Jesus said another time, "and all these things will be given to you as well" (Matthew 6:33, emphasis mine).

As I make my life about God's concerns and not my own, He will take care of the rest.

Not long after I saw that wild little "bike girl," I made note to myself to remember that "I'm living the dream life!" I want to be like that joyriding girl, celebrating what my Father in heaven does for me each and every day.

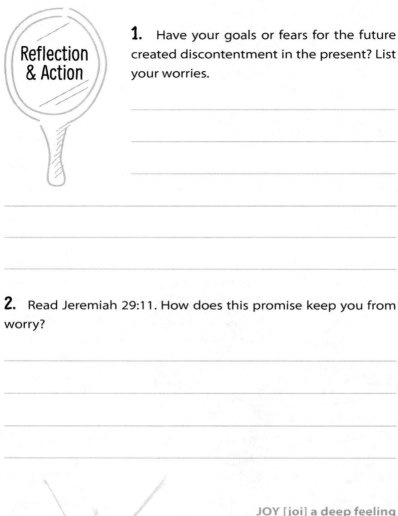

Reflection & Action

1. Have your goals or fears for the future created discontentment in the present? List your worries.

_____

_____

_____

_____

_____

_____

2. Read Jeremiah 29:11. How does this promise keep you from worry?

_____

_____

_____

_____

JOY [joi] a deep feeling
or condition of happiness
or contentment

*Cast your cares on the L<small>ORD</small> and he will sustain you;
he will never let the righteous be shaken.*
Psalm 55:22

*And we know that in all things God works for the good of those who
love him, who have been called according to his purpose.*
Romans 8:28

"Legacy"
by The Sonflowerz

"Legacy" Song Story by Becca

This song is really special and personal to us. It was written about a friend who carried the light of Christ's love into a dark corner of the earth.

We ran into Ben every week at a friend's house as we gathered to study the Bible. At one of those meetings, he shared about a missions trip he had taken to Nepal. He asked for prayer as he felt God was calling him to sell everything he had and move to this Asian nation, home of the highest point on earth, Mount Everest. His motivation was love for Jesus and the people in Nepal.

Through getting to know Ben, many people came to know

Christ. But after being there a while, Ben was suddenly killed in an accident while traveling in the mountains of Nepal. He gave his life in Nepal as a missionary, and forever changed that country and *our* lives.

It was an emotional time when we heard about Ben's sudden death. In the wake of such terrible news, Elissa picked up her guitar to soothe her own heart. But what came out was a song about an incredible life lived with outstanding devotion to God.

Later, we took the raw material of this song to Nashville, to finish it with our producer. He asked some great questions that helped us reach deeper into what the song could really communicate. We came up with a chorus that points to Jesus, who made the greatest sacrifice:

> I want to love enough to give,
> give enough to die,
> die enough to live my life
> for such a sacrifice.

Every time we play "Legacy," it moves my heart to remember Ben—and to live for God to the fullest! (Check out our music video of this song to see footage of Ben in Nepal, at www.sonflowerz .com)

Day 19
Drama Queen

by Elissa

There were days when I was the sister you didn't want to be around. I called them "drama queen days." I'm sure I made Becca sometimes wonder if Cheetos were likely to be thrown across the room!

When I was younger, these intense emotions came out around friends. Look out! They called me "moody" or "melodramatic." Either way, I've never been afraid to express how I feel.

A drama queen is a person
who often has exaggerated
or overly emotional reactions
to events or situations.

But this drama was not what God intended for me. You know that thing called "self-control"? That is what I needed to acquire.

We are all at risk of drama—outbursts of selfishness or anger—causing trouble and conflict for those around us. It's what the Bible calls our "flesh" or "sinful nature" showing up! Jesus has called us to "walk by the Spirit," which is the exact opposite of our "flesh." You'll know when you are living by the Spirit, because the fruit of the Spirit shows up instead: love, joy, peace, patience, kindness, goodness, faith, gentleness, and self-control (Galatians 5:22–23). Notice that *love* is at the top of the list! You've probably heard it before, but a drama-crazy life can be remedied with this: "Love your neighbor as yourself."

What drama have you instigated within your close relationships?

JOT IT DOWN:

_____

_____

_____

_____

_____

_____

_____

_____

_____

_____

On my most dramatic days, if you had sat me down and told me these things it may have only frustrated me more! Of course, I wanted to love people—but how? Trying to measure up to a list of rules doesn't work. "What matters is faith working through love" (Galatians 5:6 HCSB).

God's Spirit—you know, the One who lives inside us when we accept Christ—is there to bring peace into every square inch of our lives.

One of the Bible's great prophets, Isaiah, explained what God's Spirit is meant to do in us when we entrust ourselves to Jesus. "You will guard him and keep him in perfect and constant peace whose mind [both its inclination and its character] is stayed on You, because he commits himself to You, leans on You, and hopes confidently in You" (Isaiah 26:3 AMP).

Picture a sturdy apple tree reaching to the sky, its branches stretching out and bearing large, juicy red apples. Now, what if you cut off a branch? Can you expect to find lovely apples on that branch next season? Nope. In order to bear fruit, the branch has to remain on the tree. Jesus gave a similar example in John 15:1–5. He is the vine (or tree!) and we are the branches. We need to stay connected to Jesus—in our heart, mind, and spirit—if we are going to see good fruit in our lives.

My "Drama Queen" days feel like a distant memory, because God has changed me so profoundly. He gave me the grace I needed to follow Him day by day. His Spirit guided me into His love, and showed me how to love others in return. Now, it's just as fun to be around me as it is my sister!

God's grace is here for you, as well. Drama doesn't have to define us!

Reflection & Action

1. Are *you* the drama queen? (Come on. Be honest!) Read John 15:7–8. Write a prayer about your desire to be a true disciple of Christ.

_____

_____

_____

_____

_____

_____

_____

_____

_____

2. Take a minute to pray for the relationships in your life that are strained by drama.

FRUIT [froot] anything produced or accruing; product, result, or effect

So letting your sinful nature control your mind
leads to death.
But letting the Spirit control your mind
leads to life and peace.
Romans 8:6 NLT

"Do not let your hearts be troubled.
You believe in God; believe also in me."
John 14:1

"Prayer for the Prodigal"
by The Sonflowerz

Day 20
Fight Like a Girl

by Becca

"It's the big thing right now!" Some of my friends were clustered around a copy of *Seventeen* magazine, poring over a long list of rules for becoming popular. Then the subject turned to which scary movie to rent and how to get a date with the hottest boy in class. I joined in, even though I knew the girls' conversation was shallow and their perspective skewed. After all, friends stick together, right?

But we just didn't see eye to eye, and before long I had to leave. Truthfully, I felt lonely in my choice to stand apart from the crowd. Following God can mean gutsy decisions to go the opposite way. And it *wasn't* easy.

Whether you realize it or not, you send a bold message to others by your choice to stand with God. My friends learned I wouldn't buckle under their peer pressure. They started leaving me out—not inviting me to that movie, or that road trip, or that sleepover. Perhaps they thought I was lame. Or maybe they knew I would speak out, and they didn't want the guilt trip.

There are defining moments in our lives, and this was one for me. Jesus said: "Enter through the narrow gate. For wide is the gate and broad is the road that leads to destruction, and many enter through it. But small is the gate and narrow the road that leads to life, and only a few find it" (Matthew 7:13–14).

So here is the question for us today: Are we up for the fight that comes with walking what Jesus calls "the narrow road"?

It's pretty simple to picture the wide road, the choices that a lot of others at school are making. They're watching the wrong kind of movies, getting too involved with boys, maybe even trying alcohol. It takes guts to say "no" to those things, and walk the narrow road instead.

What kind of peer pressure have you dealt with?

DESCRIBE IT:

A lot of girls feel conflicted over issues like:

- How they should dress
- How much they should weigh
- Lying to their parents
- Wanting the trendy stuff their friends have
- Hanging out with people they're not comfortable with

I can go down this list and think of a time (or several times) when I wrestled with a choice. Lie to my parents, or tell them the truth? Wear what's popular, or think about the message I'm sending? And the list could go on.

If it weren't for God's Spirit, I wouldn't have lasted long on the narrow road. You can't see Him with your eyes, but He's the One who lives inside you as your source of strength to stand up for what you know is right. Have you realized your need for Him lately? I have.

> You and I were made
> for so much more
> than following the whims
> of those around us.

A friend of mine, author Vicki Courtney, says, "Self-control, apart from the power of Christ, is futile." This means that my willpower will eventually fail! It's only God's help in my life that enables me to stand up to every kind of peer pressure.

Believe me, you and I were made for so much more than following the whims of those around us. God has things in store for us that will blow our minds—but there's a catch: we gotta choose the narrow road to find them.

That moment when you are faced with a choice isn't the time to figure out how good decisions are made. You need to plan ahead, girl! So before you get to that fork in the road, here's a strategy of how to truly "fight like a girl" . . . and *win:*

Stop. Think. Pray. Three little words that pack a punch.

***Stop*—**don't jump into situations. Take a minute to make a right-on decision.

***Think*—**consider the implications and what the Bible lays out for you. (Read it regularly so verses come to mind!)

***Pray*—**this is the key to making good choices! Prayer is essentially asking God to guide you. Then trust Him to show you what to do. He *will* give you a way out.

In 2 Peter 1:6, Peter, an extraordinary leader in the early church, sums up the formula for self-control: Knowing God leads to self-control. Self-control leads to patient endurance, and patient endurance leads to godliness. Essentially, self-control is a byproduct of knowing God—and it's a result of the Spirit living inside you (Galatians 5:22–23)!

So who is guiding your decisions? Do your more outgoing friends make your choices for you? Girls with a take-charge attitude tend to influence their friends, for good or bad. If you're happy taking a back seat and letting others lead the way, you could be giving into peer pressure without knowing it. But if you're the girl who is naturally prone to leadership, make sure you are first taking orders from the greatest Leader, Jesus Christ.

Every one of you has the opportunity to lead. Show your friends—show everyone—what it looks like to walk the narrow road.

Reflection & Action

1. People who follow Jesus, trying to live like Him, are described in Hebrews 11:13 as "strangers on earth." Have you embraced this identity, or are you trying to be like the world around you?

_____

_____

_____

_____

_____

_____

_____

2. Today, when faced with a challenging choice, put "**Stop, Think, and Pray"** into practice.

3. Read Matthew 26:41 and pray for God's strength and wisdom when you are tempted.

NAR·ROW [nair-oh] including or involving a small number of things or people

Blessed are those who find wisdom,
those who gain understanding,
for she is more profitable than silver
and yields better returns than gold.
Proverbs 3:13–14

But the wisdom that comes from heaven is first of all pure;
then peace-loving, considerate, submissive,
full of mercy and good fruit,
impartial and sincere.
James 3:17

"We Depend on You"
by The Sonflowerz

Day 21
Sister vs. Sister

by Becca

I once had an unforgettable conversation with a friend who had started a band with her sisters at the same time we did.

We were on the deck of a beautiful home overlooking the grand mountain range surrounding Vail, Colorado. Breathtaking. The hosts had a history with my friend's parents and I jumped at the invitation to join them on vacation.

We discussed the intertwining of sisterhood and band life. Comparisons and careless remarks between sisters can create divisions of the worst kind. My friend confided that God had been asking her to shut the door on envy.

Through her confession, God had a message for my heart too. My friend told me to embrace my own role in the band, never becoming envious of my sister's role or gifts. Everything inside me knew she was right. It was a pivotal moment.

In our family, I was the star soccer player and the outgoing person. But starting a band with my sister meant I had to be more of a team player. I couldn't fight for center stage. That weekend I said a simple prayer, expressing my heart to God. "I'm giving this to you," I said. "I need your grace and strength to be satisfied in the role you have given me. I choose to be humble, to serve, to work as a team, and to do it ultimately for your glory, not mine."

Envy creeps in subtly, beginning with thoughts like, "I wish I had what she has," or, "She doesn't deserve that as much as I do." But at its core, envy is accusing God of not providing what we need. We look at what others have and feel dissatisfied with our own portion. It's weighing our "have nots" with their "haves."

Any situation can breed discontent when we let our focus drift from what God has given us to what He's given other people. Girls, let's be aware of what's going on in the corridors of our hearts—"let us not become conceited, provoking and envying each other" (Galatians 5:26).

What is one way you can avoid wanting what your friends or siblings have?

I'm a decorating fanatic—and always hanging posters on my wall. One has on it the words of 1 Corinthians 13, the chapter of the Bible most famous for describing perfect love: "Love is patient, love is kind. It does not envy, it does not boast, it is not proud." If we are envious of our friends, we are far from loving them.

Have you let envious thoughts bully you? It's time to stand up to that thinking and make a definite switch. Envy can develop into judgment, and pretty soon you can resent your friends just for being who they are.

The reset button is love. We are all capable of pushing that button to start fresh! Before envy enters and takes root, ask God to give you love for your friends or siblings. Ask Him to show you how He's met all your needs, that happiness is not found in being like someone else or having what they have.

I've heard it said...

Love looks through a telescope; envy, through a micro-scope.

—Josh Billings

That whole weekend in Vail was thrilling, but I will always remember that conversation with my friend, whose story of overcoming envy toward her sisters resonated with me. I decided to let go too, and see sisterhood in a totally different light.

Reflection & Action

1. Write down two reasons you don't want to be envious of others.

_____

_____

_____

_____

_____

_____

_____

_____

_____

2. Confess to God any feelings of envy. Read 1 Peter 4:8 and spend time praying for any person you feel envious toward. Ask God to give you His love for them.

EN·VY [en-vee] a feeling of desire for something another person has

*Now that you have purified yourselves by obeying
the truth so that you have sincere love for each other,
love one another deeply, from the heart.*
1 Peter 1:22

*"A new command I give you:
Love one another.
As I have loved you,
so you must love one another."*
John 13:34

"God of Restoration"
by The Sonflowerz

Here are some of our favorite sister pics from growing up!
–Elissa and Becca

Day 22
70 x 7

by Elissa

Why is forgiving someone so hard? It feels like climbing uphill with the wind and rain pushing against me. Every step is a challenge, a choice. But if forgiveness is like a summit, it is more liberating than anything to reach the top.

Becca and I were talking to students at a boarding school in England when the topic of forgiveness came up. I asked the girl sitting beside me how she saw it. To her, forgiveness would be given only if someone *deserved* it.

On a day when you open your instant messages to read a nasty comment, or when a friend forgets to invite you to her party, forgiveness may be a challenge. For a split second you wish that the British girl was right—that we only have to forgive occasionally. Holding a grudge is easier, right?

Well, maybe not.

Have you ever met a truly bitter person? Negativity and discouragement eat up everything in their path. It's like a weight they swing around a room, causing destruction everywhere.

Choosing not to forgive makes bitterness fester. And festering is not a pretty thing. Medical research has even shown that bitterness can cause physical sickness, depression, anxiety, and chronic pain![1]

Have you ever held onto a grudge?
What effect did it have on your friendship
with the person you resented?

DESCRIBE:

_____

_____

_____

_____

_____

_____

_____

When I was in high school, a friend of mine found out the effects of bitterness in a very real way. She hated her dad for leaving her mom. For hours, I sat with her, talking things through—and still she wouldn't let go of her anger against her father. She ended

1   Mayo Clinic, "Forgiveness: Letting Go of Grudges and Bitterness," http://www .mayoclinic.com/ health/forgiveness/MH00131.

up with stomach ulcers and ruined relationships. Her resentment separated her from her family and left her feeling miserable. But eventually, she realized that holding the grudge hurt more than the initial reason for her anger. In time, she gave up her bitterness and began to forgive.

My friend, a daughter once distanced by hate, went to her dad for forgiveness. Like a flower about to bloom, the outcome was peace, love, and the sweetest freedom. Their relationship is strong today.

I've heard it said…

Forgiveness is to set a prisoner free, and to realize the prisoner was *you*.
—Corrie Ten Boom

To forgive someone who has harmed us is a long journey. But Jesus tells us to keep forgiving, even if it's seventy times seven times (Matthew 18:22)! That's 490 times, if you're doing the math.

Want an even better reason to forgive your greatest enemy? If for no other reason, forgive because Jesus walked a long, painful road to forgive *your* sin—including the bitterness that comes with unforgiveness! He's not focused on your record of wrongs, so why should we count the failures of others?

Do you or I deserve forgiveness? Not one bit. But Jesus forgives anyway. He wiped the slate clean for us, and never remembers our sin. I'm so amazed at this! And He sets the bar for us by saying this is what we are to do for others.

In Luke 23:34, just before His last breath on the cross, we see Jesus forgiving those who crucified Him. This depth of forgiveness is something that astounds me. Girls, it takes nothing less than God's power, working in us, to achieve it. If we commit ourselves to forgiving, allowing God to see us through to the summit, the climb will be worth every step.

Reflection & Action

1. List the names of people you need to forgive, and take a minute to pray about it.

_____

_____

_____

_____

_____

2. Read Colossians 3:12–14. What is our motivation for forgiving someone?

_____

_____

_____

_____

RE·SENT·MENT [ri-zent-muhnt]
anger, bitterness,
ill will

*Praise the L*ORD*, my soul,*
and forget not all his benefits—
who forgives all your sins
and heals all your diseases,
who redeems your life from the pit
and crowns you with love and compassion.
who satisfies your desires with good things
so that your youth is renewed like the eagle's.
Psalm 103:2–5

"And forgive us our debts,
as we also have forgiven our debtors."
Matthew 6:12

"There Is a Redeemer" by The Sonflowerz

Day 23
Defeating Depression

by Elissa

The message popped up from a teen in Michigan: "I'm pretty depressed." That same day I got a phone call from a friend who was grieving her dad's death: "I don't know what to do—I'm so depressed."

Webster's dictionary defines *depression* as "a condition of general emotional dejection and withdrawal." Depression hits different people for different reasons and stays for different amounts of time. Talk about unexpected and unwelcomed! For us girls, even the hormones in our bodies have the potential to make us feel low on certain days of the month.

Depression is a serious issue, especially for those who have hormonal or chemical imbalances. (If your feelings are extreme and long-lasting—or if you ever have thoughts of suicide—please talk to a parent, or a youth leader, or a school counselor right away.) But for many people, depression tends to be circumstantial (based on things happening around us) or spiritual (based on doubts and fears and attitudes inside us). What I'm going to say is mainly directed toward those of us who do often enjoy life . . . but find ourselves down in the dumps from time to time.

When was the last time you were depressed and why?
DESCRIBE IT:

_____

_____

_____

_____

One time I was feeling depressed due to a number of outrageous situations beyond my control. I let out a frustrated prayer in the shower (admit it—you do it too): "Ahhh! I'm so upset, God. Why can't things in life be easier?"

Honestly, I don't always hear from God every time I pray, but in that moment a fresh understanding of my situation came to me. Right in the middle of my complaining, He said, "If you would just look to my face . . ." Could seeing His face really wash away the depression my circumstances had created?

Nearly a hundred years ago, Helen Lemmel penned a song with these words:

Turn your eyes upon Jesus,
Look full in His wonderful face,
And the things of earth will grow strangely dim,
In the light of His glory and grace.

Maybe our answer is hidden there!

What does it really mean to see the face of Jesus? It means experiencing Him in such a personal way that it changes our perspective, showing us that we really do have hope. This heart-glimpse of God is also the reminder that we are not alone—Jesus is with us through the hard stuff.

The writer of Psalm 42 had hit rock bottom in his life. Listen to his desperation: "My soul thirsts for God, for the living God. When can I go and meet with God? My tears have been my food day and night, while people say to me all day long, 'Where is your God?'" (verses 2–3).

But the psalm writer then consciously turned his heart toward hope and praise:

"Why, my soul, are you downcast? Why so disturbed within me? Put your hope in God, for I will yet praise him, my Savior and my God" (verses 5, 11).

Worshiping God brings gratefulness out of our hearts. Being thankful can combat the occasional depression in our lives—even when being thankful is the *last* thing we feel like doing. God revolutionizes our hearts every time we shove the world away just to be with Him.

As girls, we sometimes can leave God out of our emotional misery when He desperately wants to be invited in!

Ten minutes spent focusing my mind and heart on God redirects my entire day. Like a good song, those moments plant seeds inside me for a future that's upbeat and cheerful.

Reflection & Action

1. List some things you are thankful for:

_____

_____

_____

_____

_____

2. What are some ways you can meet with God during a period of depression? Set up a plan for the next time you feel low.

_____

_____

_____

_____

3. I imagine Jesus' followers could have been depressed after witnessing the death of their leader and best friend. They mourned for three days, but then, Jesus rose from the dead. Their hearts were lifted *when they saw His face*. Read Luke 24:30–35.

Your fight against depression could be a spiritual one. Check out what Ephesians 6:11–17 has to say.

THANK·FUL [thangk-fuhl]
expressing gratitude
or appreciation

Hear my cry, O God;
listen to my prayer.
From the ends of the earth I call to you,
I call as my heart grows faint;
lead me to the rock that is higher than I.
For you have been my refuge,
a strong tower against the foe.
I long to dwell in your tent forever
and take refuge in the shelter of your wings.
Psalm 61:1–4

Do not be anxious about anything,
but in every situation, by prayer and petition,
with thanksgiving, present your requests to God.
And the peace of God, which transcends all understanding,
will guard your hearts and your minds in Christ Jesus.
Philippians 4:6–7

"In You Alone"
by The Sonflowerz

Day 24
Battlegrounds

by Becca

I can picture recess at my elementary school like it was yesterday. Nick, abnormally taller than everyone else in our class, spent his free time throwing verbal punches my way. He called my nine-year-old self "skinny bones." Translation? Weak. Pathetic. *Just a girl.*

Never was I more surprised than when I saw him at a Christian concert. "Hypocrite!" I said under my breath. The next day on the playground, his mean words stung even more. I *so* wanted to fight back and make him feel ashamed about how he treated me.

Each morning my mom drove Elissa and me to school, navigating jam-packed lanes of traffic on the interstate. As she piloted

our boxy grey minivan, she reminded us of the armor of God in Ephesians 6, and together we recited each line.

Imagine hearing this in our London-born mom's British accent, as you take inventory yourself: "A final word: Be strong in the Lord and in his mighty power. Put on all of God's armor so that you will be able to stand firm against all strategies of the devil. For we are not fighting against flesh-and-blood enemies, but against evil rulers and authorities of the unseen world" (Ephesians 6:10–12 NLT).

The battle I'd encountered had never been with Nick, or the catty girls at school, or any other human being. It was against the enemy of my soul, who was always trying to tear me down. Identifying my real enemy helped me to find a way to be kind at school—even maybe (just possibly!) to love my classmates as God does.

No doubt, the verses in Ephesians 6 built up my courage. I began walking into school with an invisible shield over my heart.

The inventory continues in verses 14–17, "Stand your ground, putting on the belt of truth and the body armor of God's righteousness. For shoes, put on the peace that comes from the Good News so that you will be fully prepared. In addition to all of these, hold up the shield of faith to stop the fiery arrows of the devil. Put on salvation as your helmet, and take the sword of the Spirit, which is the word of God."

Your fight may look different from the one I faced. Maybe your siblings are pointing their fingers your way. Or maybe you are bombarded by dark thoughts in your own mind. What will you do in defense?

When we acknowledge that these are real spiritual battles, and that our enemy, the devil, is behind these thoughts, we can resist them by the authority that Jesus gives us. "Submit yourselves, then, to God. Resist the devil, and he will flee from you" (James 4:7).

Have you considered the unseen spiritual battles that are being fought all around you each day? What are you doing to win those battles?

DESCRIBE IT:

_____

_____

_____

And why not invite others to join you in combat? Your trusted friends, on the same path of following Jesus, are encouragement that you're not alone in this fight. If you've been trying to overcome serious struggles on your own, maybe it's time to ask your youth pastor, your parents, or a close friend to pray with you. I guarantee, this is one of the reasons God has put them in your life!

God's Word is my sword.

My battles no longer deal with name-calling, and I haven't seen Nick in years. But I still face opposition. When I do, I remember the words of Ephesians 6. I can still picture my mom, gripping the wheel of our minivan and saying, "Now girls, let's say it together . . ."

That was years ago, but today I am prepared for any challenge because God's Word *is* my sword. My faith in Him, and His ability to overcome anything, is my shield. His Truth is secured tightly around me like a belt. The helmet of salvation protects my mind, and my heart is guarded by His righteousness!

Like it or not, this world is a battlefield. But you are perfectly protected when you take God at His word.

Reflection & Action

1. Challenge! Take a stab at memorizing Ephesians 6:10–17.

2. What is the biggest difficulty you face in your personal life? How can you stand strong according to Ephesians 6?

_____

_____

_____

_____

_____

_____

_____

_____

3. Think of two friends who struggle with personal battles, and spend a minute praying for them.

AR·MOR [ahr-mer] a covering
worn as a defense
against weapons

By myself I have sworn,
my mouth has uttered in all integrity
a word that will not be revoked:
Before me every knee will bow;
by me every tongue will swear.
They will say of me, "In the Lord alone
are deliverance and strength."
All who have raged against him
will come to him and be put to shame.
Isaiah 45:23–24

But you are a chosen people, a royal priesthood,
a holy nation, God's special possession,
that you may declare the praises of him
who called you out of darkness into his wonderful light.
1 Peter 2:9

"By Faith"
by The Sonflowerz

Day 25
The Incline

by Becca

There's a phenomenon in my city. Instead of a usual workout routine, people attempt to scale "the Incline," a long, very steep old cable car path that leads virtually *straight up* a Colorado mountainside.

It's a rite of passage for athletes at the U.S. Olympic Training Center just down the road. Beginning at about 6,500 feet in elevation, the Incline takes you to 8,500 feet in less than a mile. Rows of unevenly spaced railroad ties make it a staircase up the mountain. It's the equivalent of racing up the stairs of the Empire State Building—twice!

I feel tired just thinking about it.

Striving on our own, without God, is like running the Incline . . . with a broken leg. That's exactly how I feel some days, as I work feverishly to finish projects and accomplish things in a world where it feels like the odds are against me.

One day I finally asked God, "Where do I go from here? I feel out of breath, like I can't move forward or bear to look at the mountain ahead of me."

Do you ever feel like this?

Weakness highlights our dependence on God.

Isaiah was a prophet in the days of the Old Testament. He was called by God to speak to the people of Israel. It was an overwhelming task, but God's hand constantly supported Isaiah. Aware of his own weakness, he wrote, "Those who wait upon God get fresh strength. They spread their wings and soar like eagles, they run and don't get tired, they walk and don't lag behind" (Isaiah 40:31 MSG).

Weakness highlights our dependence on God.

Has there been a time in your life when you felt weak in your own ability?

I see my own weakness when I'm impatient with people or when I can't make good on the promise I made to a friend. I want to reach every goal I make for myself in ten seconds or less—but often find that, no matter how hard I try, those goals escape me. Whenever I feel my frailty, it is an opportunity to stop and pray.

If I'm honest, I have to admit that many of my prayers begin with frustration, with me wondering why I can't do everything with superhero strength. The truth is, I need Jesus. Desperately. He's better than anyone else at meeting needs. Far better for me to admit my weakness than climb a mountain without Him.

Just how does God's strength refresh us when we're weak?

Does it fall on us like buckets of rain in a wild storm? Or is it more like a constant, flowing river we can drink from? Could it be that we don't need a one-time deluge, but instead a daily intake of His presence?

Imagine God's strength as a pure, glistening stream, much like the ones I see in the Colorado mountains. This river of God is not going to run dry when drought hits, when we feel wrung out and used up by the tough things in life. When I reach toward this stream—God's Word that never fails me, His voice that always calms me—I am weak. But at the same time, strong (see 2 Corinthians 12:10). I confess to God that I don't have it in me—then He points to His Spirit in me and says, "Actually, yes it is in you. *I* am in you!"

Halfway up this daunting emotional Incline, I take a break to rest. My powerlessness is replaced by peace as I drink from this stream. God is strong in me in the midst of my frailty.

I've heard it said...

It's the sides of the mountains that sustain life, not the top.

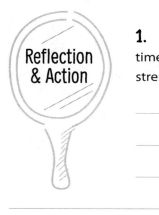

Reflection & Action

1. Read 1 Corinthians 1:25. Write about a time in your life when God became your strength.

_____

_____

_____

_____

_____

_____

_____

_____

_____

2. Next time you climb the stairs at school or take a hike with your family or friends, think about the strength God offers you in life's ups and downs.

RE·FRESH·ING [ri-fresh-ing]
serving to restore energy
and vitality

But he said to me,
"My grace is sufficient for you,
for my power is made perfect in weakness."
Therefore I will boast all the more gladly about my weaknesses,
so that Christ's power may rest on me.
2 Corinthians 12:9

You are my strength, I sing praise to you;
you, God, are my fortress,
my God on whom I can rely.
Psalm 59:17

"How Great You Are"
by The Sonflowerz

Day 26
First Response

by Elissa

Dad and Mom were newly married, living in a small town in Texas. Every night Dad drove home from his job in the city. One night Mom got a call that Dad had been in an accident, and she immediately knew that it was life-threatening.

A college student had been drinking with friends and, thinking she could make it home, took off down the pitch-black highway going the *wrong* direction. In his small Honda, Dad didn't see her car speeding toward him until the moment the pickup truck in front of him swerved off the road.

On this dark night, the first responder was a man who ran out of his nearby home at the sound of the huge crash. Because he called 911 immediately, he most likely saved my dad's life.

The drunk driver died instantly. Dad came very close, losing about 80 percent of his blood and suffering a broken jaw, femur, and left arm, as well as a crushed ankle. It took several top surgeons nine hours to piece his arm and jaw back together.

The accident happened a couple of years before I was born. I have never known Dad to walk without a limp, let alone be able to run. He has always had pain, and some days it's worse than others. Still, in all my life, I have never heard Dad respond in anger, blaming God for the accident or his pain.

We can have a lot of responses when we are at a colossal breaking point. In times when you've encountered tragedy, what has been your first response toward God?

Remember that God is not the author of pain or evil. God understands frustrated and angry prayers, and He walks with us through grief. A psalm writer said, "God is our refuge and strength, an ever-present help in trouble. Therefore, we will not fear, though the earth give way and the mountains fall into the heart of the sea, though its waters roar and foam and the mountains quake with their surging" (Psalm 46:1–3).

What circumstance represents "the earth giving way" in your life?

When the paramedics came to rescue my dad, they said it was a wonder his head and vital organs weren't injured. My grandma recalls sensing a need that day to pray for her son—and God was listening. No doubt angels were near! The doctors said it was a miracle dad survived.

Though some question God's love during tragedy, Dad became an unshakable man of faith because of his car accident. Certainly, while he spent weeks in a hospital bed, he wrestled with questions—but through it all he was convinced that God is real and loves us no matter what.

Dad says, "This side of heaven, we may never fully understand why bad things happen. Although I know every one of us has the freedom to make decisions that are good or bad, those decisions will affect others as well. For those who follow Christ, we know Romans 8:28 promises that God will ultimately work all things for good. That promise is a great comfort during hard times. In His love, God gave us free will to *choose* to love Him in return. Otherwise, we'd just be like robots to God. He doesn't want to force us to love Him, since true love is always voluntary. That's why He gives us free will."

God understands frustrated and angry prayers.

The Bible states emphatically that God is love. And in the next beat it says, "This is how God showed his love among us: He sent his one and only Son into the world that we might live through Him" (1 John 4:9). If we try to judge whether or not God loves us by a car accident or any painful circumstance, we are looking in the wrong place.

Look at the cross. God made the most extravagant sacrifice by offering Jesus' life there. It shows you that, forever and ever, He loves you. Nothing is stronger than that sacrifice and the love God has for you.

Now, how will you respond?

Reflection & Action

1. Was there a time you blamed God for a bad situation in your life? Record it here:

_____

_____

_____

_____

2. What does Jesus dying on the cross mean to you?

_____

_____

_____

3. Read Romans 8:31–37 and write out your prayer to God in response to this passage.

_____

_____

_____

REF·UGE [ref-yooj] a place or a person,
offering protection of a safe shelter
from something

But I will sing of your strength,
in the morning I will sing of your love;
for you are my fortress,
my refuge in times of trouble.
Psalm 59:16

But you, God, see the trouble of the afflicted;
you consider their grief and take it in hand.
The victims commit themselves to you;
you are the helper of the fatherless.
Psalm 10:14

"Face the Son" by The Sonflowerz

"Face the Son" Song Story by Becca

Have you ever seen a field of sunflowers? Each one follows the sun throughout the day. Their bright yellow petals just shine in the light.

Years ago when we first started our band, we played a gig in Montrose, a small town on the western slope of Colorado. We were waiting behind the stage for the signal to come on and begin. We all noticed something really strange on the stage—the person introducing us was dressed as a giant sunflower! Um, what do you do with that? Craziest start to a concert we've ever had!

The Sonflowerz has been our name from the beginning (which would explain the unique introduction in Montrose) and there's actually a deeper meaning behind it. Just like the sunflower was named for its striking resemblance to the sun, we want to be ones who take on the character of Christ in the way we love others. Like the sunflower bows its head when it's ready to spread seeds, we want to bow our hearts in worship to our Creator God. And just like the sunflower in a field will face the sun, we want to be known as people who "face the Son." And now you know the inspiration for our song!

Day 27
Courageous Beauty

by Becca

ourageous. It's a word that stirs up images of epic battle scenes like in *Avengers* or *Lord of the Rings*. Sacrifice. Perseverance. In each battle scene, the warrior fights through the fear that would try to defeat him or her.

Before you think that courage is reserved for warriors, get to know a couple friends of mine. There's Jaime, who left home to be a teacher in southeast Asia, showing God's love to Buddhist families. And there's Callie, who rides horses bareback. She can be found in our state capitol building with a passion to change politics—after feeding her horses!

Jaime and Callie will say that it wasn't easy to pursue their passions. For Jaime, living in a foreign land brought the fear of not fitting in and being alone. Callie had to devote countless hours to studying and applying for internships.

Staring fears in the face and marching into the unknown required trust in God—who is greater than anything we encounter!

Think about the most courageous thing you've ever done. Highlight some details:

_____

_____

_____

_____

_____

_____

_____

_____

Fear tells us to settle for what's easy. We've all faced it. But what we choose to do with our fear will determine our future. To live life the way God intended, we can't allow fear to paralyze us.

Esther was a girl with an extraordinary story. As an orphan Jew, she was brought up by her older cousin, Mordecai (Esther 2:5–7). Esther was gifted with incredible beauty. She found favor with the king of Persia and eventually became his queen (wow!), even though she was Jewish. During this time, Mordecai sent a message to Esther, asking her to do something courageous.

He had learned about a plot to kill the Jews. "Then on the thirteenth day of the first month the royal secretaries were summoned. . . . Dispatches were sent by couriers to all the king's provinces with the order to destroy, kill and annihilate all the Jews—young and old, women and children—on a single day" (Esther 3:12–13).

Mordecai urged Esther to go to the king on the Jews' behalf. Esther's royal status didn't erase the fears churning inside her. She told her cousin (this is my Becca translation), "I haven't been allowed to see the king for a month. You know that if I show up without an invitation, I could be killed!" Riddled with fear, she didn't want to break protocol and complete the assignment God was giving her.

Can you relate to Esther? Um, my hand is raised! Truth is, when I'm on stage, fear shouts in my mind: You're unqualified! You'll sound ridiculous! But the craziest part is that I can sense God speaking over all the noise, calming my fears every time I step out.

Mordecai told Esther, "Who knows but that you have come to your royal position for such a time as this?" (Esther 4:14). His words convicted her, and well aware that she needed God's favor if she was to succeed, she bravely asked Mordecai to organize a time of fasting for her. "When this is done," she said, "I will go to the king, even though it is against the law. And if I perish, I perish" (Esther 4:16). The end of the story is that the king granted her request, and "there was joy and gladness among the Jews, with feasting and celebrating" (Esther 8:17). Esther's faith and courage saved her people.

I've heard it said...

Feed your fears and your faith will starve. Feed your faith, and your fears will.
—Max Lucado

Faith in God makes us courageous. We hang on to these words: "Since God assured us, 'I'll never let you down, never walk off and leave you,' we can boldly quote, 'God is there, ready to help; I'm fearless no matter what. Who or what can get to me?'" (Hebrews 13:6 MSG).

Faith is the exact opposite of fear. At some point, we will all be confronted with something we feel unprepared for. But God wants us to take on these challenges, so our faith in Him can rise to the occasion.

Jaime and Callie provide inspiration for living courageously. Girls, it's time to do battle with fear. What's your bold move?

Reflection & Action

1. Is there a particular fear that keeps you from saying "yes" to the things God has called you to do?

2. Define *faith* in your own words:

_____

_____

_____

_____

_____

_____

_____

3. Read Hebrews 11. What stands out to you the most?

_____

_____

_____

_____

_____

_____

COUR·AGE [kur-idj] the ability to do
something difficult or dangerous;
mental or moral strength

"So do not fear, for I am with you;
do not be dismayed, for I am your God.
I will strengthen you and help you;
I will uphold you with my righteous right hand."
Isaiah 41:10

"Have I not commanded you?
Be strong and courageous.
Do not be afraid;
do not be discouraged,
for the Lᴏʀᴅ your God will be with you wherever you go."
Joshua 1:9

"All Over the World"
by The Sonflowerz

Day 28
Between the Songs

by Becca

I know a guy who just drools over his car. His Nissan Altima Coupe, to be specific. Even in the extreme winter, it stays polished to show off the metallic slate paint job. I might even go so far as to say this guy worships his car.

Why? Whether we know it or not, everyone worships something. Not everyone's into Nissans. It could be the new iPhone, a boy band, the latest TV show, or money.

For us girls, one culprit might be that perfect appearance we spend hours pursuing in front of the mirror, or the popularity we sacrifice everything to have. We become worshipers of anything that consumes our time and thoughts.

I used to think worshiping God was something we did on Sunday mornings—you know, just before the pastor speaks. But I've discovered that a music service just scratches the surface of worship. In reality, God invites us to ditch the other distractions and worship Him between the songs. Every day of the week.

A while back I was hanging out at a friend's house. A group of us were chatting about our summer plans when someone turned on the TV and a tasteless show started. The conversation halted, and I felt convicted. *Should I say something?* I felt my heart pound as I weighed the reactions that might follow. *If I step out, people would call me a wimp,* I thought, *or holier-than-thou.* I was fighting an internal battle, debating whether to please people or honor God. I knew what we were watching did not enable us to worship Him.

I had a choice to make. *Speak out!* was the urging my heart responded to. So I went for it. Collecting every power within to find a loving, humble way, I asked my friend if she would change the channel. Yeah, she wasn't thrilled.

But here's the conviction I had elected to live with: "A time will come, however, indeed it is already here, when the true (genuine) worshipers will worship the Father in spirit and in truth (reality); for the Father is seeking just such people as these as His worshipers" (John 4:23 AMP).

> Bringing authentic worship to God isn't easy when we have to go against the flow—the opposite way from what feels comfortable to us.

When have you ever felt this way?
Write down a time when you were reluctant to go against what everyone else was doing but made a stand anyway.

_____

_____

_____

_____

If you think about it, worshiping God and loving Him are tied together. His unconditional love for us activates a response of worship within us. Our thoughts and actions then serve as the main avenue by which our love for God moves.

Sooner or later you will be confronted with a choice. You'll be in a situation where you'll need to demonstrate courage if your words and actions are to reveal God. What will you choose?

I've heard it said...

We must never rest until everything inside us worships God.
—A. W. Tozer

Our hearts were not meant to worship temporary things. That Nissan Coupe will turn to rust someday. Popularity will come and go. The TV show will become outdated. I can't even compare those things to Jesus, who is always worthy of my worship, forever. This will never change! Then why do we choose to worship other things?

It isn't just the songs you sing that express worship to God. Throughout the week, God is looking for your whole heart. Your attention. Your _response_. Today, let God's ever-present love for you be the fuel for your worship!

Reflection & Action

1. What do you worship? For my friend, it's his car. What first comes to mind for you?

_____

_____

_____

_____

2. Read Psalm 19:14. In your own words, ask God to help you live a life of devotion to Him no matter what.

3. Write down three areas of your life where you desire to bring God worship. Given your unique circumstances, be specific about what this worship can look like.

_____

_____

_____

_____

_____

WORSHIP [wuhr-ship] love and honor
shown to God; the act of showing
love and honor to God

All the nations you have made
will come and worship before you, Lord;
they will bring glory to your name.
For you are great and do marvelous deeds;
you alone are God.
Psalm 86:9–10

Therefore, I urge you, brothers and sisters,
in view of God's mercy,
to offer your bodies as a living sacrifice,
holy and pleasing to God—
this is your true and proper worship.
Romans 12:1

"My Adoration" by The Sonflowerz

Day 29
Cooking Up Compassion

by Becca

My head was pressed against the window of the van as we drove into the slums of El Salvador. It was my first face-to-face experience with extreme poverty. I had come with the Christian children's ministry Compassion International to give supplies to churches and hug my very own sponsor child. As I stepped out of the van, the sun's heat pounded down and unfamiliar, musty smells filled the air.

There in the alley I met Stephanie, an eighteen-year-old who had recently lost her mother in a tragic accident. Desperately trying to fix their leaky roof in a storm, Stephanie's mother slipped and fell to her death. Stephanie looked like someone who could have gone to school with me—instead, she was raising her sisters and brothers by herself, in a house with no running water and a makeshift fireplace for a kitchen.

My heart broke for her. I forgot all about the heat.

Where I come from, a day without electricity is a rare inconvenience (and a huge one, if I'm honest). But for Stephanie, pure water is hard to come by. I was compelled to reach out to her with the compassion of God in any way I could. God was working a change in my heart.

I will never live the same since that day I stepped off the plane in El Salvador. I saw so much hopelessness, pain, and dirt! I adopted a radically different view of what compassion looks like. Instead of being all about me, God changed my perspective to an others-centered, love-driven focus.

This transformation in me was inspired by the life of Jesus. He gave us a clear description of what God thinks about suffering and difficulty in the world—like the kind I saw firsthand in El Salvador.

It was Jesus who began the revolution of compassion and love.

Flip through the pages of Matthew, Mark, Luke, and John, and you will discover overwhelming accounts of Jesus's undeniable sympathy and compassion. What did He think about the multitudes of people who were hungry, broken, and diseased? "When Jesus . . . saw a large crowd, he had compassion on them and healed their sick" (Matthew 14:14).

Then Jesus encountered two blind men on the side of the road, and He "had compassion on them and touched their eyes" (Matthew 20:34). And even on the cross, bearing incredible pain on our account, He saw His mother, Mary, and told one of His disciples to take care of her (John 19:25–27).

His concern for us is unending. As we go about our daily lives—struggling through math tests, sleepless nights, or troubling friendships—Jesus is with the Father praying for us (Romans 8:34)!

Jesus knows our personal issues, and through His loving grace He helps us to overcome. He engaged His heart in saving the lost and spent every ounce of His energy reaching out to others—including each one of us. He began the revolution of love and compassion!

Now, how can we mirror the compassion of Jesus in our own backyards?

Consider this experience from my own family: My mom used to complain that she never used her fancy bread machine enough. I longed for the smell of fresh-bread-yumminess to fill the house, but the machine just sat on the counter. Finally, one day she cracked open the lid and began preparing dough. I asked why, and was surprised by her answer.

Our neighbor two houses down had gotten the shock of her life when she found out that her husband had been robbing banks. This woman had no idea what was going on until the police came to take him to jail! Mom went to talk with our neighbor and came home with a heavy heart. Dusting off her bread machine, she went into high gear, whipping up some love. It was Mom's way of giving. Freshly baked, warm bread was delivered that evening.

In time, we moved away, but years later I ran into that neighbor. The first thing she said was how much that loaf of bread meant to her. Apparently, when the main ingredient is compassion, our gifts have a lasting effect.

In our own neighborhood or around the world, we have the chance to become the hands and feet of Jesus!

I've heard it said...

**Even when I cannot see him, I can hear the beautiful gallop of God's heartbeat for humanity.
—Christine Caine**

Reflection & Action

1. First Peter 3:8 reads, "Finally, all of you, be like-minded, be sympathetic, love one another, be compassionate and humble." What are two ways you can show compassion to those around you in a practical, tangible way?

2. How has God shown compassion to you lately?

EM·PA·THY [em-puh-thee] the power of sharing the feelings of another

The LORD is compassionate and gracious,
slow to anger, abounding in love.
Psalm 103:8

Praise be to the God and Father of our Lord Jesus Christ,
the Father of compassion and the God of all comfort,
who comforts us in all our troubles,
so that we can comfort those in any trouble
with the comfort we ourselves receive from God.
2 Corinthians 1:3–4

"The Face of Jesus" by The Sonflowerz

Day 30
Let's Get Together

by Elissa

My mom surrendered her life to Jesus when she was twenty. While visiting a friend in Kansas City, she was introduced to real church. Here's what I mean by *real:* These Midwestern "Jesus freaks" were sincere in their love for God and people, generous in their giving, and exuberant in their joy. Mom tells me she had never seen anything like it.

Growing up in England, her only exposure to religion had been singing a few hymns at her dull (and mandatory) boarding school chapels. Her first impression of "real church" in Kansas City was vastly different.

When she decided to stay for a while, this British girl found a warm Midwest welcome. New friends at the church gave her a bed, some sheets, and even a job! The love of Jesus was so tangible through the believers that she was stirred to know God. Their kindness left an impression that will last forever.

Everyone has a different opinion about church. For my mom, the experience was life-changing, and living proof that church—the people, not the building!—is a good thing when it's done right.

What are three words that you could use to describe church?

_____

_____

_____

In the Bible, the church—meaning every true Christian everywhere—is called the body of Christ. Jesus is the "Head" of the body. We are made one through Christ.

Think about it like this: "The way God designed our bodies is a model for understanding our lives together as a church: every part dependent on every other part" (1 Corinthians 12:25 MSG). When people of mixed ages, races, and backgrounds come together with love and devotion to Christ and each other, you've got church! The family of God. Lovely togetherness.

Today's culture seems to believe that virtual communication, like texting, instant messaging, Facebook, and Instagram, fulfills our need for relationships. But these virtual rituals will never replace genuine face time.

Don't you think the false sense of community we get online causes us to disengage where it matters most? I sure do. Please don't let this virtual black hole replace your "church family" time.

About two thirds of teens who attend church in high school *stop* going once they graduate, according to Barna Group.

Heading into college, some of my friends abandoned church. They just didn't think it was a worthy investment of their time, especially with their busy class schedules. Church may seem to us like an extracurricular activity, but all over the world, believers in Christ risk their lives to meet together! Their freedom to worship God is severely limited by their governments or opposing religious groups.

Most of us live on safe soil, making it easy to take church for granted. But that's a huge mistake. Church is really a dress rehearsal for eternity.

Do you ever wonder what heaven will be like? I suspect heaven is really the most outrageous church service ever. It will never be boring! Believers from every nation will worship together, and with our own eyes we will see our Savior (Revelation 7:9–10). Today, when church is done right, it can be our glimpse into heaven.

Whatever college you may attend or wherever you may move someday, finding the perfect church isn't the point. Being an active part of the body of Christ is. Without a doubt, God is calling you to this (Hebrews 10:25). If the church is a body, we need every part involved. Don't be the missing elbow or eye or hand that everyone is trying to find!

I love flipping through the photo album of my mom's first year as a believer. And it's not just because her hippie hair and bell-bottoms make me laugh. I can see, in every picture, the way church is meant to be.

Reflection & Action

1. How do these ideas change your perspective on church?

_____

_____

_____

_____

_____

_____

_____

2. Name two favorite things about your church.

_____

_____

3. Spend a minute asking God to show you how you can be involved in your church.

JE·SUS FREAK [jee-zuhss freek] a member
of the Christian youth revival, a national
movement that began in the late 1960s;
a devout Christian

Let the message of Christ dwell among you richly
as you teach and admonish one another
with all wisdom through psalms, hymns,
and songs from the Spirit,
singing to God with gratitude in your hearts.
Colossians 3:16

And let us consider how we may spur one another
on toward love and good deeds,
not giving up meeting together,
as some are in the habit of doing,
but encouraging one another—
and all the more as you see the Day approaching.
Hebrews 10:24–25

"Hallelujah to the King" by The Sonflowerz

Day 31
Made to Shine

by Elissa

Jenna peeked over the edge of a large concrete drainage ditch behind her house. "Jack! Get out of there!" she called. Her four-year-old brother had an insatiable curiosity—and Jenna was the one to chase him down this time. Jack slowly emerged and Jenna scooped him up in her arms. "Next time I'm sending Dad after you," she said, squeezing him tightly.

Walking back into the house, Jenna could hear her parents in the kitchen. They were talking with their neighbor, Mrs. Murphy. "I'm afraid to lose everything," Mrs. Murphy said in a shaky voice. Jenna stopped by the front door, letting Jack loose to run inside. Mrs. Murphy's daughter Brooke was Jenna's best friend. *Lose everything?* Jenna thought. *What does that mean?*

She darted across the street and knocked on the Murphys' door. Brooke met her there. "Are you okay?" Jenna asked. "Your mom sounds worried." Brooke stepped out to sit on the front step. "My dad lost his job yesterday and they aren't taking it very well," Brooke confided.

Jenna knew that God would be there for Brooke no matter what. But she wasn't sure Brooke knew it. A week earlier, Jenna had read in Scripture, "As I have loved you, so you must love one another. By this everyone will know that you are my disciples, if you love one another" (John 13:34–35). She wasn't sure how to love Brooke in that moment, except to listen and pray as Brooke continued to explain the situation.

Could it be, on any given day, that *this* is what shining for God looks like?

This idea of shining isn't reserved for pastors or limited to Sundays. It doesn't have to feel like a heroic act or any kind of major accomplishment. It's simply a lifestyle of knowing who you are—a daughter of God—and radiating His love to the world around you.

Jenna was shining when her brother needed some extra attention and her friend was hurting. When do *you* shine?

I've heard it said...

Even the darkest night will end and the sun will rise.

. . . .

"You're here to be light," The Message paraphrase of the Bible says, "bringing out the God-colors in the world. God is not a secret to be kept. We're going public with this, as public as a city on a hill. If I make you light-bearers, you don't think I'm going to hide you under a bucket, do you? I'm putting you on a light stand. Now that I've put you there on a hilltop, on a light stand—shine! Keep open house; be generous with your lives. By opening up to others, you'll prompt people to open up with God, this generous Father in heaven" (Matthew 5:14–16).

What I didn't tell you about Jenna is that she has a learning disability and a slight lisp. She's waiting for contacts to replace the scratched-up glasses she wears, and recently she dropped her entire lunch tray on the cafeteria floor. As you might imagine, there are classmates who keep up a constant flow of sarcastic comments and nicknames.

Shining doesn't have to feel like a heroic act or any kind of major accomplishment.

All this would have the power to devastate some girls. Well, not Jenna. She knows a million times over that God treasures her. It's there in black and white throughout God's love letters. Jenna is *made to shine*.

Evil has one purpose: to extinguish the light inside us. But God's brightest light, His very Spirit, lives inside Jenna to eliminate the darkness that tries to crowd in from outside.

That's what we wanted to say in our song "Made to Shine":

God's love is a fire inside of you,
No one can take that away.
You were made to shine a brilliant light,
To radiate His glory.
More than the stars in the night sky,
You were made to shine.

Girls, as you close this book for the final time, think of the sun on a summer day, or the full moon against the blackness of space. You have the capacity to shine brighter than these with the light of God's Spirit inside you!

Jenna is taking up a great challenge. And it's your turn now. How will you shine the God-colors of love and true life into your world?

Reflection & Action

1. Pray about this "Made to Shine" challenge. Where do you think God wants you to start or keep shining His love? Take a minute to ask Him.

_____

_____

_____

_____

_____

_____

_____

2. Write your own "Made to Shine" story. Visit our website, sonflowerz.com/madetoshine, to share it with others. You'll be spreading the light and encouraging your sisters in Christ who are also reading this book!

SHINE [shahyn] to glow or be
bright with reflected light

This is the message we have heard from him and declare to you: God is light; in him there is no darkness at all. If we claim to have fellowship with him and yet walk in the darkness, we lie and do not live out the truth. But if we walk in the light, as he is in the light, we have fellowship with one another, and the blood of Jesus, his Son, purifies us from all sin.

1 John 1:5–7

"You are the light of the world.
A town built on a hill cannot be hidden.
Neither do people light a lamp and put it under a bowl.
Instead they put it on its stand,
and it gives light to everyone in the house.
In the same way, let your light shine before others,
that they may see your good deeds and glorify your Father in heaven."

Matthew 5:14–16

You save the humble but bring low those whose eyes are haughty.
You, LORD, keep my lamp burning;
my God turns my darkness into light.
With your help I can advance against a troop;
with my God I can scale a wall.

Psalm 18:27–29

DAILY SONG

"Made to Shine"
by The Sonflowerz

You've read the book—now what?

- Take our Made to Shine Challenge! We're asking you to get creative, and with a beautiful boldness *live out* Matthew 5:14–16. How can you radiate God's love to the world around you?

- Share your Shine story and it will encourage others to do the same!

- Watch our video message to you and check out other Shine stories. Visit sonflowerz.com/madetoshine.

- Comment about your favorite devotional in the book and tell us why. Write to us: team@sonflowerz.com.

Made to Shine Events

- Visit The Sonflowerz online to check out our music and find out how you can bring a *Made to Shine* event to your hometown!

Many Thanks

To Mom and Dad for cheering us on, being examples of Christ's light, and showing us the way. Our husbands for the amazing love and support we needed to write our best. Our editor, Paul Muckley, for doing such a great job and making us better writers. Susie Shellenberger and Vicki Courtney, thank you for your friendship and your example. Paige Green, Amy Cato, and Michelle Hicks—much of our inspiration for this book came from *You & Your Girl*. To CharisYouth and all of the girls in our lives who inspire us to keeping shining. We love you!